(I'd really struggle without God)

Selections from
The Living Bible

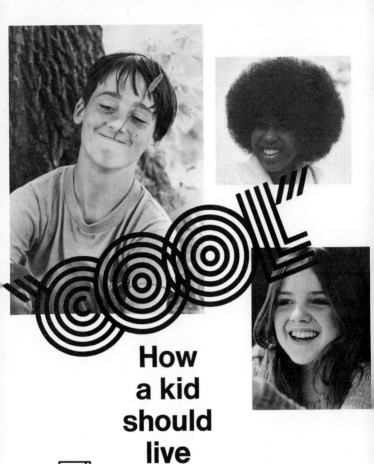

COOL

How a kid should live

Tyndale House Publishers, Inc.
Wheaton, Illinois

Coverdale House
Publishers, Ltd.
London, England

All Scripture passages
are from *The Living Bible*,
paraphrased by Kenneth N. Taylor,
© 1971 by Tyndale House Publishers.

This book is different in more ways than one.

First, it is not a book for you to sit down and read until you are tired of reading. Instead, it is a book for you to read *every day,* one page at a time.

Second, it is not a book written by a person. It is a book written by God, so it should be read carefully. Ask God to speak to you as you read, telling you how he wants you to think and to live in these important days.

At the bottom of every page there are blank lines. Use these spaces for:

> —a record of God's special word to you that day
>
> —a diary
>
> —prayer requests
>
> —birthday reminders or special events in your life

It's a cool life—when you live it the way God wants you to.

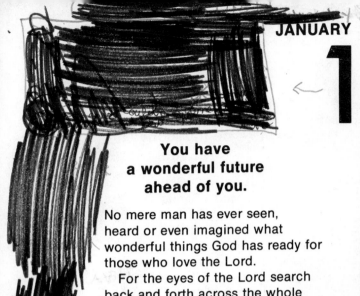

You have
a wonderful future
ahead of you.

No mere man has ever seen, heard or even imagined what wonderful things God has ready for those who love the Lord.

For the eyes of the Lord search back and forth across the whole earth, looking for people whose hearts are perfect toward him, so that he can show his great power in helping them.

Don't let anyone think little of you because you are young. Be their ideal . . . be a pattern for them in your love, your faith, and your clean thoughts.

Be delighted with the Lord. Then he will give you all your heart's desires.

TODAY

Proverbs 23:17, 18. 1 Corinthians 2:9. 2 Chronicles 16:9. 1 Timothy 4:12. Psalm 37:4.

JANUARY

2

Understand who Christ is and all that he has done for you.

God's Son shines out with God's glory, and all that God's Son is and does marks him as God. He regulates the universe by the mighty power of his command. He is the one who died to cleanse us and clear our record of all sin, and then sat down in highest honor beside the great God of heaven. Thus he became far greater than the angels, as proved by the fact that his name "Son of God," which was passed on to him from his Father, is far greater than the names and titles of the angels.

Far, far above any other king or ruler or dictator or leader. Yes, his honor is far more glorious than that of anyone else either in this world or in the world to come.

TODAY

Ephesians 1:17.   Hebrews 1:3, 4.   Ephesians 1:21.

**Jesus,
our leader
and
instructor.**

"I am the A and the Z, the Beginning and the Ending of all things," says God, who is the Lord, the All Powerful One who is, and was, and is coming again!

Who has done such mighty deeds, directing the affairs of generations of mankind as they march by? It is I, the Lord, the First and Last; I alone am he.

God who began the good work within you will keep right on helping you grow in his grace until his task within you is finally finished on that day when Jesus Christ returns.

TODAY

Hebrews 12:2.   Revelation 1:8.   Isaiah 41:4.   Philippians 1:6.

JANUARY

4

Put on the armor of right living.

Ask the Lord Jesus Christ to help you live as you should.

He will accept and acquit us—declare us "not guilty"—if we trust Jesus Christ to take away our sins. And we all can be saved in this same way, by coming to Christ, no matter who we are or what we have been like.

For though once your heart was full of darkness, now it is full of light from the Lord, and your behavior should show it! Take no part in the worthless pleasures of evil and darkness, but instead, rebuke and expose them. When you expose them, the light shines in upon their sin and shows it up, and when they see how wrong they really are, some of them may even become children of light!

TODAY

Romans 13:12. Romans 13:14. Romans 3:22. Ephesians 5:8, 11, 13.

Follow God's example in everything you do.

Be full of love for others, following the example of Christ who loved you and gave himself to God as a sacrifice to take away your sins. And God was pleased, for Christ's love for you was like sweet perfume to him.

Dirty stories, foul talk and coarse jokes—these are not for you. Instead, remind each other of God's goodness and be thankful.

You can be sure of this: The kingdom of Christ and of God will never belong to anyone who is impure or greedy, for a greedy person is really an idol worshiper—he loves and worships the good things of this life more than God.

TODAY

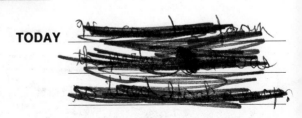

Ephesians 5:1. Ephesians 5:2, 4, 5.

6

Just as you trusted Christ to save you, trust him, too, for each day's problems.

See that you go on growing in the Lord, and become strong and vigorous in the truth you were taught. Let your lives overflow with joy and thanksgiving for all he has done.

Don't let others spoil your faith and joy with their philosophies, their wrong and shallow answers built on men's thoughts and ideas, instead of on what Christ has said.

Most of all, let love guide your life.

TODAY

Colossians 2:6. Colossians 2:7. Colossians 2:8

Stop being mean, bad-tempered and angry. Quarreling, harsh words, and dislike of others should have no place in your lives

Stop lying to each other; tell the truth . . . when we lie to each other we are hurting ourselves.

If you are angry, don't sin by nursing your grudge. Don't let the sun go down with you still angry—get over it quickly.

If anyone is stealing he must stop it.

Don't use bad language. Say only what is good and helpful to those you are talking to.

Be kind to each other, tenderhearted, forgiving one another, just as God has forgiven you because you belong to Christ.

TODAY

Ephesians 4:31. Ephesians 4:25, 26, 28, 29, 32.

JANUARY

Wednesday

8

There are
three things that remain—
faith, hope, and love—
and the greatest of these
is love.

Love is very patient and kind,
never jealous or envious, never
boastful or proud, never haughty or
selfish or rude. Love does not
demand its own way. It is not
irritable or touchy. It does not
hold grudges.

It is never glad about injustice,
but rejoices whenever truth wins
out. If you love someone you will
be loyal to him no matter what the
cost.

All the special gifts and powers
from God will someday come to
an end, but love goes on forever.

So see to it that you really do
love each other warmly, with all
your hearts.

TODAY

1 Corinthians 13:13. 1 Corinthians 13:4, 5, 6, 7, 8. 1 Peter 1:22.

. . . **Love
makes up
for many
of your faults.**

I [Jesus] am giving a new
commandment to you now—love
each other just as much as I love
you.

Don't repay evil for evil. Don't
snap back at those who say
unkind things about you. Instead,
pray for God's help for them, for
we are to be kind to others, and
God will bless us for it.

Love overlooks insults.

Let us stop just *saying* we love
people; let us *really* love them, and
show it by our *actions.* Then we
will know for sure, by our actions,
that we are on God's side, and
our consciences will be clear, even
when we stand before the Lord.

TODAY

1 Peter 4:8. John 13:34. 1 Peter 3:9. Proverbs 10:12. 1 John 3:18, 19.

Friday

JANUARY

10

**Help me,
undeserving as I am,
to obey your laws,
for I have chosen
to do right.**

I cling to your commands and
follow them as closely as I can.
Lord, don't let me make a mess of
things.

If you will only help me to want
your will, then I will follow your
laws even more closely.

Just tell me what to do and I
will do it, Lord. As long as I live I'll
wholeheartedly obey.

Make me walk along the right
paths for I know how delightful
they really are.

Turn me away from wanting
any other plan than yours.

TODAY

Psalm 119:29. Psalm 119:30, 31, 32, 33, 34, 35, 37.

**God showed
his great love for us
by sending Christ
to die for us
while we were
still sinners.**

And since by his blood he did
all this for us as sinners, how
much more will he do for us now
that he has declared us not
guilty? Now he will save us from
all of God's wrath to come. And
since, when we were his enemies,
we were brought back to God by
the death of his Son, what
blessings he must have for us
now that we are his friends, and he
is living within us!

Now we rejoice in our wonderful
new relationship with God—all
because of what our Lord Jesus
Christ has done in dying for our
sins—making us friends of God.

TODAY

Romans 5:8. Romans 5:9, 10, 11.

Sunday

JANUARY

12

**Listen to
your father
and mother.**

Tie their instructions around your finger so you won't forget. Take to heart all of their advice. Every day and all night long their counsel will lead you and save you from harm; when you wake up in the morning, let their instructions guide you into the new day.

For their advice is a beam of light directed into the dark corners of your mind to warn you of danger and to give you a good life.

TODAY

Proverbs 1:8. Proverbs 6:21, 22, 23.

The Lord is coming soon.

The Lord himself will come down from heaven with a mighty shout and with the soul-stirring cry of the archangel and the great trumpet-call of God. And the believers who are dead will be the first to rise to meet the Lord. Then we who are still alive and remain on the earth will be caught up with them in the clouds to meet the Lord in the air and remain with him forever.

While you are waiting for these things to happen and for him to come, try hard to live without sinning; and be at peace with everyone so that he will be pleased with you when he returns.

TODAY

Philippians 4:5.   1 Thessalonians 4:16, 17.   2 Peter 3:14.

JANUARY

14

**As long as
the earth remains,
there will be
springtime
and harvest . . .
winter
and summer.**

The earth belongs to God.
Everything in all the world is his!

He sends the snow in all its
lovely whiteness, and scatters the
frost upon the ground.

But then he calls for warmer
weather, and the spring winds blow
and all the river ice is broken.

He covers the heavens with
clouds, sends down the showers
and makes the green grass grow in
mountain pastures.

He sends peace across your
nation, and fills your barns with
plenty of the finest wheat.

TODAY _____

Genesis 8:22. Psalm 24:1. Psalm 147:16, 18, 8, 14.

O Lord my God, how great you are!

You stretched out the starry curtain of the heavens, and hollowed out the surface of the earth to form the seas.

You bound the world together so that it would never fall apart. You spoke, and at the sound of your shout the water collected into its vast ocean beds, and mountains rose and valleys sank to the levels you decreed.

There before me lies the mighty ocean, teeming with life of every kind, both great and small. And look! See the ships! And over there, the whale you made to play in the sea.

TODAY

Psalm 104:1. Psalm 104:2, 3, 5, 7, 8, 25, 26.

Thursday

God looked over all that he had made, and it was excellent in every way.

He placed springs in the valleys, and streams that gush from the mountains. They give water for all the animals to drink. There the wild donkeys quench their thirst, and the birds nest beside the streams and sing among the branches of the trees.

The Lord planted the cedars of Lebanon. They are tall and flourishing. There the birds make their nests, the storks in the firs. High in the mountains are pastures for the wild goats, and rock-badgers burrow in among the rocks and find protection there.

TODAY

Genesis 1:31. Psalm 104:10, 11, 12, 16, 17, 18.

Seek the Lord and live.

Seek him who created the Seven
Stars and the constellation Orion,
who turns darkness into morning,
and day into night, who calls
forth the water from the ocean and
pours it out as rain upon the
land. The Lord, Jehovah, is his
name.

Get to know the God of your
fathers. Worship and serve him
with a clean heart and a willing
mind, for the Lord sees every
heart and understands and knows
every thought. If you seek him,
you will find him.

TODAY

Amos 5:6, 8. 1 Chronicles 28:9.

**You may be
sure that your sin
will catch up with you.**

Your sins have cut you off from
God. Because of sin he has
turned his face away from you and
will not listen anymore. Your sins
keep piling up before the righteous
God . . . waiting to attack you,
longing to destroy you.

But if we confess our sins to
him, he can be depended on to
forgive us and to cleanse us
from every wrong.

Create in me a new, clean
heart, O God, filled with clean
thoughts and right desires.

TODAY

Numbers 32:23.   Isaiah 59:2, 12.   Genesis 4:7.   1 John 1:9.   Psalm 51:10.

Sunday

JANUARY

19

Fill up any little cracks there may yet be in your faith.

In a wealthy home there are dishes made of gold and silver as well as some made from wood and clay. The expensive dishes are used for guests, and the cheap ones are used in the kitchen or to put garbage in.

If you stay away from sin you will be like one of these dishes made of purest gold—the very best in the house—so that Christ himself can use you for his highest purposes.

Have faith and love, and enjoy the companionship of those who love the Lord and have pure hearts.

This will result in your hearts being made strong, sinless and holy by God our Father, so that you may stand before him guiltless on that day when our Lord Jesus Christ returns with all those who belong to him.

TODAY

1 Thessalonians 3:10.   2 Timothy 2:20, 21, 22.   1 Thessalonians 3:13.

Nicodemus . . . came secretly to interview Jesus.

Even many of the Jewish leaders believed him to be the Messiah but wouldn't admit it to anyone.

The Holy Spirit, God's gift, does not want you to be afraid of people, but to be wise and strong, and to love them and enjoy being with them. If you will stir up this inner power, you will never be afraid to tell others about our Lord.

If anyone publicly acknowledges me [Jesus] as his friend, I will openly acknowledge him as my friend before my Father in heaven.

TODAY

John 7:50. John 12:42. 2 Timothy 1:7, 8. Matthew 10:32.

21

Jesus is truly the Son of God.

We know he is, because God said so with a voice from heaven when Jesus was baptized, and again as he was facing death—yes, not only at his baptism but also as he faced death. And the Holy Spirit, forever truthful, says it too. So we have these three witnesses:

> the voice of the Holy Spirit in our hearts
> the voice from heaven at Christ's baptism, and
> the voice before he died.

And they all say the same thing: that Jesus Christ is the Son of God.

We believe men who witness in our courts, and so surely we can believe whatever God declares.

TODAY

1 John 5:5.   1 John 5:6, 7, 8, 9.

Wednesday

**Those who do
what Christ tells them to
will learn to love God
more and more.**

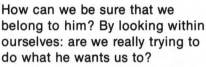

How can we be sure that we
belong to him? By looking within
ourselves: are we really trying to
do what he wants us to?

If we stay close to him, obedient
to him, we won't be sinning
either; but as for those who keep
on sinning, they should realize
this: They sin because they have
never really known him or
become his.

As we live with Christ, our love
grows more perfect and complete;
so we will not be ashamed and
embarrassed at the day of
judgment, but can face him with
confidence and joy, because he
loves us and we love him too.

TODAY

1 John 2:5.   1 John 2:3.   1 John 3:6.   1 John 4:17.

Treat others as you want them to treat you.

Do you think you deserve credit for merely loving those who love you? Even the godless do that! And if you do good only to those who do you good—is that so wonderful? Even sinners do that much!

And if you lend money only to those who can repay you, what good is that? Even the most wicked will lend to their own kind for full return!

Love your *enemies!* Do good to *them!* Lend to *them!* And don't be concerned about the fact that they won't repay. Then your reward from heaven will be very great, and you will truly be acting as sons of God.

TODAY

Luke 6:31. Luke 6:32, 33, 34, 35.

The rhinoceros has such bad eyesight that it cannot even see what it is running after.

If you have good eyesight and good hearing, thank God who gave them to you.

Then God said, "Let us make a man—someone like ourselves, to be the master of all life upon the earth and in the skies and in the seas."

You [God] made all the delicate, inner parts of my body, and knit them together in my mother's womb. Thank you for making me so wonderfully complex! You saw me before I was born and scheduled each day of my life before I began to breathe.

Everything we have has come from you, and we only give you what is yours already.

TODAY

Proverbs 20:12.   Genesis 1:26.   Psalm 139:13, 14, 16.   1 Chronicles 29:14.

**Watch your tongue!
Keep your lips from lying.**

Telling lies about someone is as harmful as hitting him with an axe, or wounding him with a sword, or shooting him with a sharp arrow.

If you want a happy, good life, keep control of your tongue, and guard your lips from telling lies. Turn away from evil and do good. Try to live in peace even if you must run after it to catch and hold it! For the Lord is watching his children, listening to their prayers; but the Lord's face is hard against those who do evil.

TODAY

Psalm 34:13.　Proverbs 25:18.　1 Peter 3:10, 11, 12.

**Evil men and false teachers
will become worse and worse . . .
But you must keep on
believing the things
you have been taught.**

Beware of false teachers who
come disguised as harmless
sheep, but are wolves and will tear
you apart.

You can detect them by the way
they act, just as you can identify
a tree by its fruits.

Not all who sound religious are
really godly people. They may refer
to me as "Lord," but still won't
get to heaven. For the decisive
question is whether they obey
my Father in heaven.

TODAY

2 Timothy 3:13, 14. Matthew 7:15, 16, 21.

Turn me away from wanting any other plan than yours.

Do you want more and more of God's kindness and peace? Then learn to know him better and better.

For as you know him better, he will give you, through his great power, everything you need for living a truly good life.

You need more than faith; you must also work hard to be good, and even that is not enough. For then you must learn to know God better and discover what he wants you to do.

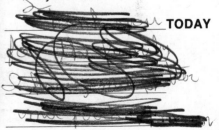

TODAY

Psalm 119:37. 2 Peter 1:2, 3, 5.

Tuesday

JANUARY

28

I can't make myself do right.
I want to but I can't.

If we say that we have no sin,
we are only fooling ourselves,
and refusing to accept the truth.

The Lord looks down from
heaven on all mankind to see if
there are any who are wise, who
want to please God. But no, all
have strayed away; all are rotten
with sin.

But to all who received him,
he gave the right to become
children of God. All they needed to
do was to trust him to save them

TODAY

Romans 7:18. 1 John 1:8. Psalm 14:2, 3. John 1:12.

Wednesday

JANUARY

29

The apostles told [Jesus] all they had done.

Don't worry about anything;
instead, pray about everything;
tell God your needs and don't
forget to thank him for his
answers.

We should behave like God's
very own children . . . calling to
him, "Father, Father."

Everything he has belongs to us,
for that is the way God planned.

So let us come boldly to the very
throne of God and stay there to
receive his mercy and to find grace
to help us in our times of need.

TODAY

Mark 6:30. Philippians 4:6. Romans 8:15. Galatians 4:7. Hebrews 4:16.

30

Nothing can be hidden from him to whom we must explain all that we have done.

He knows about everyone, everywhere. Everything about us is bare and wide open to the all-seeing eyes of our living God.

Whatever God says to us is full of living power: it is sharper than the sharpest dagger, cutting swift and deep into our innermost thoughts and desires with all their parts, exposing us for what we really are.

If you sin, there is someone to plead for you before the Father. His name is Jesus Christ, the one who is all that is good and who pleases God completely.

TODAY

Hebrews 4:13b. Hebrews 4:13a, 12. 1 John 2:1.

Friday

JANUARY

31

**Throw
yourself
into your tasks
so that everyone
may notice your
improvement
and progress.**

Be sure that everything is done
properly in a good and orderly way.

This should be your ambition:
to live a quiet life, minding your
own business and doing your own work.

Listen to your father's advice
and don't despise an old mother's
experience. Get the facts at any
price, and hold on tightly to all the
good sense you can get.

Give your parents joy!

TODAY

1 Timothy 4:15. 1 Corinthians 14:40. 1 Thessalonians 4:11. Proverbs 23:22, 23, 25.

God looks at our motives.

The Lord watches over all the
plans and paths of godly men,
but the paths of the godless lead
to doom.

The Lord will show you who are
his, and who is holy.

Your Father who knows all
secrets will reward you.

Search me, O God, and know my
heart; test my thoughts. Point
out anything you find in me that
makes you sad, and lead me
along the path of everlasting life.

We need have no fear of
someone who loves us perfectly;
his perfect love for us eliminates
all dread of what he might do to
us.

TODAY

Proverbs 21:2.   Psalm 1:6.   Numbers 16:5.   Matthew 6:4.   Psalm 139:23, 24.
1 John 4:18.

Sunday

FEBRUARY

2

**Be beautiful inside,
in your hearts,
with the lasting charm
of a gentle
and quiet spirit
which is so precious
to God.**

For you have a new life. It was
not passed on to you from your
parents, for the life they gave you
will fade away. This new one will
last forever, for it comes from
Christ, God's ever-living Message
to men.

Anyone who believes in me
[Jesus], even though he dies like
anyone else, shall live again.

Our earthly bodies which die
and decay are different from the
bodies we shall have when we
come back to life again, for they
will never die.

TODAY

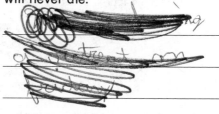

1 Peter 3:4. 1 Peter 1:23. John 11:25. 1 Corinthians 15:42.

**God . . .
is the one
who invited you into
this wonderful friendship
with his Son,
even Christ
our Lord.**

See how very much our heavenly
Father loves us, for he allows us
to be called his children.

Follow God's example in
everything you do just as a much
loved child imitates his father.

Since we are his children, we will
share his treasures—for all God gives
to his Son Jesus is now ours too.

Keep your eyes on Jesus, our
leader and instructor. He was
willing to die a shameful death on
the cross because of the joy he
knew would be his afterwards; and
now he sits in the place of
honor by the throne of God.

 **TODAY**

1 Corinthians 1:9. 1 John 3:1. Ephesians 5:1. Romans 8:17. Hebrews 12:2.

Tuesday

FEBRUARY

4

The God who looked upon me.

O Lord, you have examined my heart and know everything about me. You know when I sit or stand. When far away you know my every thought. You chart the path ahead of me, and tell me where to stop and rest. Every moment, you know where I am.

You spread out our sins before you—our secret sins—and see them all.

He knows about everyone, everywhere. Everything about us is bare and wide open to the all-seeing eyes of our living God; nothing can be hidden from him to whom we must explain all that we have done.

TODAY

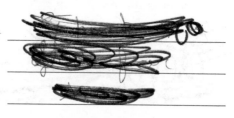

Genesis 16:13. Psalm 139:1, 2, 3. Psalm 90:8. Hebrews 4:13.

I will give you a new heart.

I will give you new and right desires—and put a new spirit within you. I will take out your stony hearts of sin and give you new hearts of love.

The Lord is good and glad to teach the proper path to all who go astray; he will teach the ways that are right and best to those who humbly turn to him. And when we obey him, every path he guides us on is fragrant with his lovingkindness and his truth.

Live and act in a way worthy of those who have been chosen for such wonderful blessings as these. Be humble and gentle. Be patient with each other, making allowance for each other's faults because of your love.

TODAY

Ezekiel 36:26. Psalm 25:8, 9, 10. Ephesians 4:1, 2.

**Don't get into
needless fights.**

For there are six things the Lord
hates—no, seven:
    Haughtiness
     Lying
      Murdering
       Plotting evil
        Eagerness to do wrong
        A false witness
         Sowing discord among
          brothers

    Obey your father and your
mother. Their advice is a beam
of light directed into the dark
corners of your mind to warn
you of danger and to give you a
good life.

TODAY _____

_____

_____

Proverbs 3:30. Proverbs 6:16, 17, 18, 19, 20, 23.

**Be kind to each other,
tenderhearted,
forgiving one another,
just as God
has forgiven you
because you belong
to Christ.**

Share each other's troubles and
problems, and so obey our
Lord's command.

Give to those who ask, and
don't turn away from those who
want to borrow.

When others are happy, be happy
with them. If they are sad, share
their sorrow.

Don't let anyone think little of
you because you are young. Be
their ideal; let them follow the
way you teach and live; be a
pattern for them in your love,
your faith, and your clean thoughts.

TODAY _____

_____

_____

Ephesians 4:32. Galatians 6:2. Matthew 5:42. Romans 12:15. 1 Timothy 4:12.

**Don't do
your good deeds publicly,
to be admired,
for then you will lose
the reward from your Father
in heaven.**

When you give a gift to a beggar, don't shout about it as the hypocrites do—blowing trumpets in the synagogues and streets to call attention to their acts of charity! I tell you in all earnestness, they have received all the reward they will ever get.

But when you do a kindness to someone, do it secretly—don't tell your left hand what your right hand is doing. And your Father who knows all secrets will reward you.

TODAY _____

_____

_____

_____

_____

Matthew 6:1. Matthew 6:2, 3, 4.

I will give you leaders
after my own heart,
who will guide you
with wisdom and
understanding.

Honor the officers of your
church who work hard among
you and warn you against all that
is wrong. Think highly of them
and give them your wholehearted
love because they are straining
to help you.

Think of all the good that has
come from their lives, and try to
trust the Lord as they do.

Pray . . . for kings and all others
who are in authority over us, or
are in places of high responsibility.

_____ **TODAY**

_____

_____

Jeremiah 3:15.   1 Thessalonians 5:12, 13.   Hebrews 13:7.   1 Timothy 2:2.

FEBRUARY

10

**Bring others
to Christ.
Leave nothing
undone that you
ought to do.**

"O Lord God," I said, "I can't do that! I'm far too young! I'm only a youth!" "Don't say that," he replied, "for you will go wherever I send you and speak whatever I tell you to. And don't be afraid of the people, for I, the Lord, will be with you and see you through."

Go directly to the Father and ask him, and he will give you what you ask for because you use my name. You haven't tried this before, [but begin now]. Ask, using my name, and you will receive, and your cup of joy will overflow.

You can get anything—*anything* you ask for in prayer—if you believe.

TODAY _____

_____

2 Timothy 4:5. Jeremiah 1:6, 7, 8. John 16:23, 24. Matthew 21:22.

**The Lord is fair
in everything he does,
and full of kindness.
He is close to all
who call on him sincerely.**

Jabez . . . prayed to the God of
Israel, "Oh, that you would
wonderfully bless me and help me
in my work; please be with me
in all that I do, and keep me from
all evil and disaster!" And God
granted him his request.

God appeared to Solomon and
told him, "Ask me for anything,
and I will give it to you."
Solomon replied, "O God . . . give
me wisdom and knowledge to
rule . . . properly, for who is able
to govern by himself such a
great nation as this one of yours?"

God gave Solomon great
wisdom and understanding. His
wisdom excelled that of any of
the wise men of the East.

TODAY _____

_____

_____

Psalm 145:17, 18.   1 Chronicles 4:9, 10.   2 Chronicles 1:7, 8, 10.   1 Kings 4:29, 30.

FEBRUARY

12

The Lord grants wisdom.

His every word is a treasure of knowledge and understanding. He grants good sense to the godly—his saints. He is their shield, protecting them and guarding their pathway. He shows how to distinguish right from wrong, how to find the right decision every time.

He alone is God, and full of wisdom.

TODAY _____

_____

_____

Proverbs 2:6.   Proverbs 2:7, 8, 9, 10.   1 Timothy 1:17.

Don't look
to men for help;
their greatest leaders fail.

For every man must die. His
breathing stops, life ends, and in
a moment all he planned for
himself is ended.

But happy is the man who has
the God of Jacob as his helper,
whose hope is in the Lord his
God—the God who made both
earth and heaven, the seas and
everything in them. He is the
God who keeps every promise.

I will be your God through all
your lifetime, yes, even when your
hair is white with age.

_____ **TODAY**

_____

_____

Psalm 146:3. Psalm 146:4, 5, 6. Isaiah 46:4.

FEBRUARY
14

Have two goals: wisdom—that is, knowing and doing right— and common sense.

Don't let them slip away, for they fill you with living energy, and are a feather in your cap.

I would have you learn this great fact: that a life of doing right is the wisest life there is. If you live that kind of life, you'll not limp or stumble as you run. Don't do as the wicked do. Avoid their haunts—turn away, go somewhere else. Look straight ahead; don't even turn your head to look. Watch your step. Stick to the path and be safe. Don't sidetrack; pull back your foot from danger.

Keep your eyes on Jesus, our leader and instructor. Let God train you.

TODAY _____

_____

_____

Proverbs 3:21a. Proverbs 3:21b, 22. Proverbs 4:11, 12, 14, 15, 25, 26, 27.
Hebrews 12:2, 7.

FEBRUARY
15

God is
with us.

If God is on our side, who can
ever be against us?

He is for me. How can I be
afraid? What can mere man do
to me?

The Lord is my light and my
salvation; whom shall I fear? Yes,
though a mighty army marches
against me, my heart shall know no
fear. I am confident that God will
save me.

God is with us; he is our
Leader.

The Commander of the armies
of heaven is here among us.

TODAY _____

_____

_____

Isaiah 8:10. Romans 8:31. Psalm 118:6. Psalm 27:1, 3. 2 Chronicles 13:12.
Psalm 46:7.

**You can sleep without fear;
you need not be afraid
of disaster . . .
for the Lord is with you;
he protects you.**

As evening fell, Jesus said to his disciples, "Let's cross to the other side of the lake."

Soon a terrible storm arose. High waves began to break into the boat until it was nearly full of water and about to sink. Jesus was asleep at the back of the boat with his head on a cushion. Frantically they wakened him, shouting, "Teacher, don't you even care that we are all about to drown?" Then he rebuked the wind and said to the sea, "Quiet down!" And the wind fell, and there was a great calm!

Don't worry about anything; instead, pray about everything; tell God your needs and don't forget to thank him for his answers.

I will lie down in peace and sleep, for though I am alone, O Lord, you will keep me safe.

TODAY _____

_____

_____

Proverbs 3:24, 25, 26. Mark 4:35, 37, 38, 39. Philippians 4:6. Psalm 4:8.

FEBRUARY

17

**The Lord guided them
by a pillar of cloud
during the daytime,
and by a pillar of fire
at night.**

Your words are a flashlight to
light the path ahead of me, and
keep me from stumbling.
  I will instruct you (says the
Lord) and guide you along the best
pathway for your life; I will
advise you and watch your
progress. Don't be like a
senseless horse or mule that has to
have a bit in its mouth to keep
it in line!
  And when we obey him, every
path he guides us on is fragrant
with his lovingkindness and his truth
  Show me the path where I
should go, O Lord; point out the
right road for me to walk.

_____ **TODAY**

_____

_____

Exodus 13:21. Psalm 119:105. Psalm 32:8, 9. Psalm 25:10, 4.

Quietly trust yourself to Christ your Lord.

Do what is right; then if men speak against you, calling you evil names, they will become ashamed of themselves for falsely accusing you when you have only done what is good.

Praise the Lord if you are punished for doing right! Of course, you get no credit for being patient if you are beaten for doing wrong; but if you do right and suffer for it, and are patient beneath the blows, God is well pleased.

Be beautiful inside, in your hearts, with the lasting charm of a gentle and quiet spirit which is so precious to God.

TODAY _____

_____

_____

1 Peter 3:15. 1 Peter 4:16. 1 Peter 2:19, 20. 1 Peter 3:4.

Always be fair and honest.

Daniel soon proved himself more capable than all the other presidents and governors, for he had great ability, and the king began to think of placing him over the entire empire as his administrative officer.

This made the other presidents and governors very jealous, and they began searching for some fault in the way Daniel was handling his affairs so that they could complain to the king about him. But they couldn't find anything to criticize! He was faithful and honest, and made no mistakes.

So Daniel prospered.

Listen to what the Lord is saying. He has told you what he wants, and this is all it is: *to be fair and just and merciful and to walk humbly with your God.*

Do things in such a way that everyone can see you are honest clear through.

_____ **TODAY**

_____

_____

Ezekiel 45:9.   Daniel 6:3, 4, 28.   Micah 6:1, 8.   Romans 12:17.

FEBRUARY

20

The character of even a child can be known by the way he acts— whether what he does is pure and right.

I would have you learn this great fact: that a life of doing right is the wisest life there is. If you live that kind of life, you'll not limp or stumble as you run.

Follow God's example in everything you do. Be full of love for others, following the example of Christ who loved you and gave himself to God as a sacrifice to take away your sins. And God was pleased, for Christ's love for you was like sweet perfume to him. Though once your heart was full of darkness, now it is full of light from the Lord, and your behavior should show it!

_____ **TODAY**

_____

_____

Proverbs 20:11. Proverbs 4:11, 12. Ephesians 5:1, 2, 8.

FEBRUARY

21

Pray . . . for kings and all others who are in authority over us, or are in places of high responsibility, so that we can live in peace and quietness, spending our time in godly living and thinking much about the Lord.

This is good and pleases God our Savior, for he longs for all to be saved and to understand this truth:

That God is on one side and all the people on the other side, and Christ Jesus, himself man, is between them to bring them together, by giving his life for all mankind.

Pray much for others.

TODAY _____

_____

_____

1 Timothy 2:1.   1 Timothy 2:2, 3, 4, 5, 6.

FEBRUARY

22

Ask the Lord Jesus Christ to help you live as you should.

If someone mistreats you because you are a Christian, don't curse him; pray that God will bless him. When others are happy, be happy with them. If they are sad, share their sorrow. Work happily together. Don't try to act big. Don't try to get into the good graces of important people, but enjoy the company of ordinary folks. And don't think you know it all.

Never pay back evil for evil. Do things in such a way that everyone can see you are honest clear through. Don't quarrel with anyone. Be at peace with everyone, just as much as possible.

TODAY _____

_____

_____

_____

_____

_____

Romans 13:14.   Romans 12:14, 15, 16, 17, 18.

The Lord is on my side.

Remember this—the wrong desires that come into your life aren't anything new and different. Many others have faced exactly the same problems before you. And no temptation is irresistible. You can trust God to keep the temptation from becoming so strong that you can't stand up against it, for he has promised this and will do what he says. He will show you how to escape temptation's power so that you can bear up patiently against it.

If God is on our side, who can ever be against us?

He is for me! How can I be afraid? What can mere man do to me?

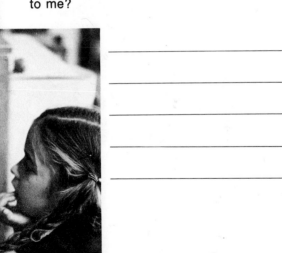

_____ **TODAY**

_____

_____

_____

_____

Psalm 118:7. 1 Corinthians 10:13. Romans 8:31. Psalm 118:6.

FEBRUARY

24

My help is from Jehovah who made the mountains! And the heavens too!

Just as the mountains surround and protect Jerusalem, so the Lord surrounds and protects his people.

He protects you day and night. He keeps you from all evil, and preserves your life. He keeps his eye upon you as you come and go, and always guards you.

O God enthroned in heaven, I lift my eyes to you. We look to Jehovah our God for his mercy and kindness just as a servant keeps his eyes upon his master or a slave girl watches her mistress for the slightest signal.

My eyes are ever looking to the Lord for help, for he alone can rescue me.

Our help is from the Lord who made heaven and earth.

TODAY _____

_____

_____

Psalm 121:2. Psalm 125:2. Psalm 121:6, 7, 8. Psalm 123:1, 2. Psalm 25:15.
Psalm 124:8.

**I pray
that you will begin
to understand
how incredibly great
his power is to help
those who believe him.**

It is that same mighty power that
raised Christ from the dead and
seated him in the place of honor at
God's right hand in heaven, far,
far above any other king or ruler or
dictator or leader. Yes, his honor
is far more glorious than that of
anyone else either in this world
or in the world to come. And God
has put all things under his feet
and made him the supreme Head
of the church—which is his
body, filled with himself, the Author
and Giver of everything
everywhere.

TODAY _____

_____

_____

Ephesians 1:19. Ephesians 1:20, 21, 22, 23.

26

Abraham never doubted. He believed God, for his faith and trust grew ever stronger.

Abraham still trusted in God and his promises, and so he offered up his son Isaac, and was ready to slay him on the altar of sacrifice; yes, to slay even Isaac, through whom God had promised to give Abraham a whole nation of descendants! He believed that if Isaac died God would bring him back to life again.

He was completely sure that God was well able to do anything he promised.

Is anything too hard for God?

TODAY _____

_____

_____

Romans 4:20. Hebrews 11:17, 18, 19. Romans 4:21. Genesis 18:14.

Men of God in days of old were famous for their faith.

It was by faith that Abel obeyed God and brought an offering that pleased God more than Cain's offering did. God accepted Abel and proved it by accepting his gift; and though Abel is long dead, we can still learn lessons from him about trusting God.

Noah was another who trusted God. When he heard God's warning about the future, Noah believed him even though there was then no sign of a flood, and wasting no time, he built the ark and saved his family.

These men of faith . . . were living for heaven. And now God is not ashamed to be called their God, for he has made a heavenly city for them.

TODAY _____

_____

_____

Hebrews 11:2.   Hebrews 11:4, 7, 13, 16.

FEBRUARY

28

It is the confident assurance that something we want is going to happen. It is the certainty that what we hope for is waiting for us, even though we cannot see it up ahead.

By faith—by believing God—we know that the world and the stars—in fact, all things—were made at God's command; and that they were all made from things that can't be seen.

You can never please God without faith, without depending on him. Anyone who wants to come to God must believe that there is a God and that he rewards those who sincerely look for him.

TODAY _____

_____

_____

Hebrews 11:1. Hebrews 11:3, 6.

What is faith?

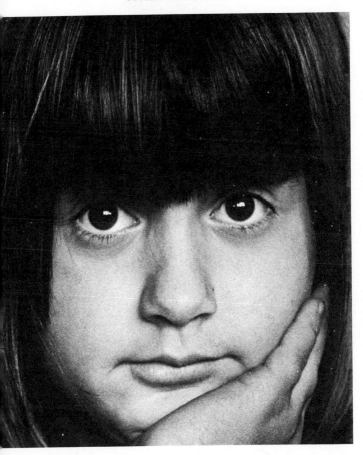

FEBRUARY
29

**God gives strength
to the humble,
but sets himself
against the proud
and haughty.**

So give yourselves humbly to
God. Resist the devil and he will
flee from you. And when you draw
close to God, God will draw
close to you. Wash your hands, you
sinners, and let your hearts be
filled with God alone to make them
pure and true to him.

Let there be tears for the wrong
things you have done. Let there
be sorrow and sincere grief. Let
there be sadness instead of
laughter, and gloom instead of joy.
Then when you realize your
worthlessness before the Lord, he
will lift you up, encourage and help you.

TODAY _____

_____

_____

James 4:6.   James 4:7, 8, 9, 10.

There is not
a single man
in all the earth
who is always good
and never sins.

As the Scriptures say, "No one is good—no one in all the world is innocent."

No one has ever really followed God's paths, or even truly wanted to.

Every one has turned away; all have gone wrong. No one anywhere has kept on doing what is right; not one.

Now do you see it? No one can ever be made right in God's sight by doing what the law commands. For the more we know of God's laws, the clearer it becomes that we aren't obeying them.

Yet now God declares us "not guilty" of offending him if we trust in Jesus Christ, who in his kindness freely takes away our sins.

TODAY _____

_____

_____

Ecclesiastes 7:20. Romans 3:10, 11, 12, 20, 24.

MARCH

2

**This Good News
was promised long ago
by God's prophets
in the Old Testament.**

It is the Good News about his Son, Jesus Christ our Lord, who came as a human baby, born into King David's royal family line; and by being raised from the dead he was proved to be the mighty Son of God, with the holy nature of God himself.

And now, through Christ, all the kindness of God has been poured out upon us undeserving sinners.

This Good News tells us that God makes us ready for heaven—makes us right in God's sight—when we put our faith and trust in Christ to save us. This is accomplished from start to finish by faith. As the Scripture says it, "The man who finds life will find it through trusting God."

TODAY _____

_____

_____

Romans 1:2.   Romans 1:3, 4, 5, 17.

**If you believe
that Jesus is the Christ
that he is God's Son
and your Savior—
then you are a child of God.**

And all who love the Father love
his children too. So you can find
out how much you love God's
children—your brothers and
sisters in the Lord—by how much
you love and obey God. Loving
God means doing what he tells us
to do, and really, that isn't hard
at all; for every child of God can
obey him, defeating sin and evil
pleasure by trusting Christ to help
him.

But who could possibly fight and
win this battle except by
believing that Jesus is truly the Son
of God?

TODAY _____

_____

_____

1 John 5:1a.   1 John 5:1b, 2, 3, 4, 5.

MARCH

4

Jesus the Son of God is our great High Priest.

Jesus Loves you

Chris Harrison, age 8

Therefore let us never stop trusting him. This High Priest of ours understands our weaknesses, since he had the same temptations we do, though he never once gave way to them and sinned. So let us come boldly to the very throne of God and stay there to receive his mercy and to find grace to help us in our times of need.

For the Lord is always good. He is always loving and kind, and his faithfulness goes on and on.

_____ **TODAY**

_____

_____

Hebrews 4:14a.   Hebrews 4:14b, 15, 16.   Psalm 100:5.

God's marvelous love . . . so great that you will never see the end of it or fully know or understand it.

You know how full of love and kindness our Lord Jesus was: though he was so very rich, yet to help you he became so very poor, so that by being poor he could make you rich.

Since God loved us as much as that, we surely ought to love each other too.

Be kind to each other, tenderhearted, forgiving one another, just as God has forgiven you because you belong to Christ.

Be gentle and ready to forgive; never hold grudges. Remember, the Lord forgave you, so you must forgive others.

TODAY _____

_____

_____

Ephesians 3:17, 19.   2 Corinthians 8:9.   1 John 4:11.   Ephesians 4:32.   Colossians 3:13.

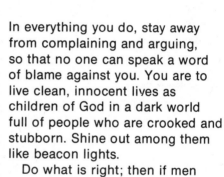

**If someone mistreats you
because you are a Christian,
don't curse him;
pray that God
will bless him.**

In everything you do, stay away
from complaining and arguing,
so that no one can speak a word
of blame against you. You are to
live clean, innocent lives as
children of God in a dark world
full of people who are crooked and
stubborn. Shine out among them
like beacon lights.

Do what is right; then if men
speak against you, calling you evil
names, they will become
ashamed of themselves for falsely
accusing you when you have
only done what is right.

TODAY _____

_____

_____

Romans 12:14. Philippians 2:14, 15. 1 Peter 3:16.

Love your *enemies!* Pray for those who *persecute* you!

The Jewish leaders were stung to fury by Stephen's accusation, and ground their teeth in rage. But Stephen, full of the Holy Spirit, gazed steadily upward into heaven and saw the glory of God and Jesus standing at God's right hand.

Then they mobbed him, putting their hands over their ears, and drowning out his voice with their shouts, and dragged him out of the city to stone him.

And as the murderous stones came hurtling at him, Stephen prayed, "Lord Jesus, receive my spirit." And he fell to his knees, shouting, "Lord, don't charge them with this sin!" and with that, he died.

TODAY

Matthew 5:44. Acts 7:54, 55, 57, 58, 59, 60.

MARCH

8

When the Holy Spirit controls our lives he will produce . . . patience, kindness.

Be humble and gentle. Be patient with each other, making allowances for each other's faults because of your love.

Be kind to each other, tenderhearted, forgiving one another, just as God has forgiven you because you belong to Christ.

You are living a brand new kind of life that is continually learning more and more of what is right, and trying constantly to be more and more like Christ who created this new life within you.

Yes, be patient. And take courage, for the coming of the Lord is near.

TODAY _____

_____

_____

Galatians 5:22. Colossians 3:10. Galatians 6:9. James 5:8.

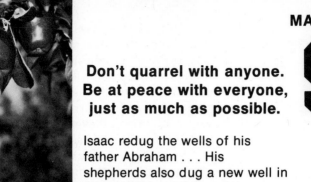

Don't quarrel with anyone. Be at peace with everyone, just as much as possible.

Isaac redug the wells of his father Abraham . . . His shepherds also dug a new well in Gerar Valley, and found a gushing underground spring. Then the local shepherds came and claimed it. "This is our land and our well," they said, and argued over it with Isaac's herdsmen. So he named the well, "The Well of Argument!" Isaac's men then dug another well, but again there was a fight over it. So he called it, "The Well of Anger." Abandoning that one, he dug again, and the local residents finally left him alone.

Let us not get tired of doing what is right, for after a while we will reap a harvest of blessing if we don't get discouraged and give up.

Never pay back evil for evil.

TODAY _____

_____

_____

Romans 12:18. Genesis 26:18, 19, 20, 21, 22. Galatians 6:9. Romans 12:17.

**Watch for
my return!**

The day of the Lord is surely
coming . . . then the heavens
will pass away with a terrible noise
and the heavenly bodies will
disappear in fire, and the earth and
everything on it will be burned up.

However, no one, not even the
angels in heaven, nor I myself,
knows the day or hour when
these things will happen; only the
Father knows. And since you
don't know when it will happen,
stay alert. Be on the watch.

He isn't really being slow about
his promised return, even though
it sometimes seems that way. But
he is waiting, for the good
reason that he is not willing that
any should perish, and he is
giving more time for
sinners to repent.

TODAY _____

_____

_____

2 Peter 3:9.

As the Scriptures say, "No one is good—no one in all the world is innocent."

No one has ever really followed God's paths, or even truly wanted to.

Every one has turned away; all have gone wrong. No one anywhere has kept on doing what is right; not one.

God says he will accept and acquit us—declare us "not guilty"—if we trust Jesus Christ to take away our sins. And we all can be saved in this same way, by coming to Christ, no matter who we are or what we have been like.

Each of us will stand personally before the Judgment Seat of God.

TODAY _____

_____

_____

Romans 14:10. Romans 3:10, 11, 12, 22.

MARCH

12

**The Lord
our God,
the Almighty,
reigns.**

God can do what men can't.

He does whatever he thinks
best among the hosts of heaven, as
well as here among the
inhabitants of earth. No one can
stop him or challenge him,
saying, "What do you mean by
doing these things?"

From eternity to eternity I am
God. No one can oppose what I
do.

Father, Father . . . everything
is possible for you.

I know that you can do
anything.

TODAY _____

_____

_____

Revelation 19:6. Luke 18:27. Daniel 4:35. Isaiah 43:13. Mark 14:36. Job 42:2.

**Your steadfast love, O Lord,
is as great as all the heavens.
Your faithfulness reaches
beyond the clouds.**

He is merciful and tender toward
those who don't deserve it; he is
slow to get angry and full of
kindness and love. He never
bears a grudge, nor remains angry
forever. He has not punished us
as we deserve for all our sins, for
his mercy toward those who fear
and honor him is as great as the
height of the heavens above the
earth. He has removed our sins as
far away from us as the east is
from the west. He is like a father
to us, tender and sympathetic to
those who reverence him.

TODAY _____

_____

_____

Psalm 36:5.   Psalm 103:8, 9, 10, 11, 12, 13.

MARCH

14

Who is Jehovah?

I alone am God. There is no other God; there never was and never will be. I am the Lord, and there is no other Savior.

I called you by name when you didn't know me. What right have you to question what I do? Who are you to command me concerning the work of my hands? I have made the earth and created man upon it. With my hands I have stretched out the heavens and commanded all the vast myriads of stars.

Let all the world look to me for salvation! For I am God; there is no other. Every knee in all the world shall bow to me, and every tongue shall swear allegiance to my name.

TODAY _____

Exodus 5:2. Isaiah 43:1, 11. Isaiah 45:4, 11, 12, 22, 23.

There is none like the God of Jerusalem.

The voice of the Lord echoes from the clouds. The God of glory thunders through the skies. So powerful is his voice; so full of majesty.

He merely spoke, and the heavens were formed, and all the galaxies of stars. He made the oceans, pouring them into his vast reservoirs. When he but spoke, the world began! It appeared at his command!

Who else but God goes back and forth to heaven? Who else holds the wind in his fists, and wraps up the oceans in his cloak? Who but God has created the world? If there is any other, what is his name?

_____ **TODAY**

_____

Deuteronomy 33:26. Psalm 29:3, 4. Psalm 33:6, 7, 9. Proverbs 30:4.

At the Flood, the Lord showed his control

of all creation.

The crime rate was rising rapidly
across the earth, and, as seen by
God, the world was rotten to the
core.

As God observed how bad it was,
and saw that all mankind was
vicious and depraved, he said to
Noah, " . . . Look! I am going to
cover the earth with a flood and
destroy every living being—
everything in which there is
the breath of life. All will die.

"But I promise to keep you safe
in the ship, with your wife and
your sons and their wives."

The curse of God is on the
wicked, but his blessing is on the
upright.

_____ **TODAY**

_____

_____

Psalm 29:10.   Genesis 6:11, 12, 17, 18.   Proverbs 3:33.

**God carefully watches
the goings on
of all mankind;
he sees them all.**

Woe to those who try to hide
their plans from God, who try to
keep him in the dark concerning
what they do! "God can't see
us," they say to themselves. "He
doesn't know what is going on!"

How stupid can they be! Isn't he,
the Potter, greater than you, the
jars he makes? Will you say to
him, "He didn't make us"? Does
a machine call its inventor dumb?

TODAY

_____

_____

_____

Job 34:21. Isaiah 29:15, 16.

Being a fool makes you a blabbermouth.

It is far better not to say you'll do something than to say you will and then not do it.

Dreaming instead of doing is foolishness, and there is ruin in a flood of empty words; fear God instead.

So when you talk to God and vow to him that you will do something, don't delay in doing it, for God has no pleasure in fools. Keep your promise to him.

And I tell you this, that you must give account on Judgment Day for every idle word you speak.

_____**TODAY**

_____

_____

Ecclesiastes 5:3.   Ecclesiastes 5:5, 7, 4.   Matthew 12:36.

Keep your ears open and your mouth shut!

Don't be a fool who doesn't even realize it is sinful to make rash promises to God, for he is in heaven and you are only here on earth, so let your words be few.

Don't ever forget that it is best to listen much, speak little, and not become angry.

Not all who sound religious are really godly people. They may refer to me as "Lord," but still won't get to heaven. For the decisive question is whether they obey my Father in heaven.

All who listen to my instructions and follow them are wise.

The crowds were amazed at Jesus' sermons, for he taught as one who had great authority.

TODAY _____

_____

_____

Ecclesiastes 5:1.   Ecclesiastes 5:2, 3.   James 1:19.   Matthew 7:21, 24, 28, 29.

Create in me a new, clean heart,
O God, filled with clean thoughts
and right desires. Make me willing
to obey you.

How can I ever know what sins
are lurking in my heart? Cleanse
me from these hidden faults. And
keep me from deliberate wrongs;
help me to stop doing them.

May my spoken words and
unspoken thoughts be pleasing
even to you, O Lord my Rock
and my Redeemer.

**Lord,
don't let
me make
a mess
of things.**

TODAY _____

_____

_____

Psalm 119:31.   Psalm 51:10, 12.   Psalm 19:12, 13, 14.

Help me to prefer obedience.

Blessed Lord, teach me your
rules. I have recited your laws,
and rejoiced in them more than
in riches. I will meditate upon them
and give them my full respect. I
will delight in them and not
forget them.

Bless me with life so that I
can continue to obey you. Open my
eyes to see wonderful things in
your Word. I am but a pilgrim here
on earth: how I need a map—
and your commands are my
chart and guide.

Billy Powell, age 9

TODAY _____

_____

_____

Psalm 119:36. Psalm 119:12, 13, 14, 15, 16, 17, 18, 19.

MARCH

22

Every law of God is right.

God's laws are perfect. They protect us, make us wise, and give us joy and light.

God's laws are pure, eternal, just. They are more desirable than gold. They are sweeter than honey dripping from a honeycomb.

Fix your thoughts on what is true and good and right. Think about things that are pure and lovely, and dwell on the fine, good things in others. Think about all you can praise God for and be glad about.

What a God he is! How perfect in every way! All his promises prove true. He is a shield for everyone who hides behind him. For who is God except our Lord? Who but he is as a rock?

_____ **TODAY**

_____

_____

Psalm 119:128. Psalm 19:7, 8, 9, 10. Philippians 4:8. Psalm 18:30, 31.

Whatever God says to us is full of living power.

It is sharper than the sharpest dagger, cutting swift and deep into our innermost thoughts and desires with all their parts, exposing us for what we really are. He knows about everyone, everywhere. Everything about us is bare and wide open to the all-seeing eyes of our living God; nothing can be hidden from him to whom we must explain all that we have done.

Today if you hear God's voice speaking to you, do not harden your hearts against him.

TODAY _____

_____

_____

Hebrews 4:12a.   Hebrews 4:12b, 13.   Hebrews 3:15.

MARCH

24

**You have
been given freedom:
not freedom to do wrong,
but freedom to love
and serve each other.**

For the whole Law can be
summed up in this one
command: "Love others as you
love yourself."

But if instead of showing love
among yourselves you are always
critical and catty, watch out!
Beware of ruining each other.

I advise you to obey only the
Holy Spirit's instructions. He will
tell you where to go and what to
do, and then you won't always be
doing the wrong things your evil
nature wants you to.

For we naturally love to do evil
things that are just the opposite
from the things that the Holy Spirit
tells us to do.

_____TODAY

_____

_____

Galatians 5:13. Galatians 5:14, 15, 16, 17.

MARCH

25

**I would have you
learn this great fact:
that a life of doing right
is the wisest life there is.**

But when you follow your own
wrong inclinations your lives will
produce these evil results:
impure thoughts . . .
hatred and fighting,
jealousy and anger,
constant effort to get the
best for yourself,
complaints and criticisms,
the feeling that everyone
else is wrong except those
in your own little group.
Let me tell you . . . anyone
living that sort of life will not
inherit the kingdom of God.

TODAY _____

_____

_____

Proverbs 4:11. Galatians 5:19, 20, 21.

Teach us to number our days . . . help us to spend them as we should.

Be careful how you act; these are difficult days. Don't be fools; be wise: make the most of every opportunity you have for doing good.

Obey all of the commandments . . . Love the Lord and follow his plan for your lives. Cling to him and serve him enthusiastically.

Work hard to prove that you really are among those God has called and chosen, and then you will never stumble or fall away. And God will open wide the gates of heaven for you to enter into the eternal kingdom of our Lord and Savior Jesus Christ.

TODAY

Psalm 90:12. Ephesians 5:15, 16. Joshua 22:5. 2 Peter 1:10, 11.

**There are many homes
up there where
my Father lives, and I am going
to prepare them
for your coming.**

The city has no need of sun or
moon to light it, for the glory of
God and of the Lamb illuminate it.
Its light will light the nations of
the earth, and the rulers of the
world will come and bring their
glory to it. Its gates never close;
they stay open all day long—and
there is no night!

Nothing evil will be permitted
in it—no one immoral or
dishonest—but only those whose
names are written in the Lamb's
Book of Life.

TODAY _____

_____

_____

John 14:2, 3. Revelation 21:23, 24, 25, 27.

MARCH

28

**Get rid of all
that is wrong
in your life,
both inside and outside.**

Be glad for the wonderful
message we have received, for it
is able to save our souls as it
takes hold of our hearts.

And remember, it is a message to
obey, not just to listen to. So
don't fool yourselves. For if a
person just listens and doesn't
obey, he is like a man looking at
his face in a mirror; as soon as
he walks away, he can't see himself
anymore or remember what he
looks like. But if anyone keeps
looking steadily into God's law
for free men, he will not only
remember it but he will do what
it says, and God will greatly bless
him in everything he does.

_____ **TODAY**

_____

_____

James 1:21. James 1:22, 23, 24, 25.

Don't worship the good things of life, for that is idolatry.

Gideon replied, " . . . I have one request. Give me all the earrings collected from your fallen foes,"—for the troops of Midian, being Ishmaelites, all wore golden earrings. "Gladly," they replied, and spread out a sheet for everyone to throw in the gold earrings he had gathered. Gideon made an ephod from the gold and put it in Ophrah, his home town. But all Israel soon began worshiping it, so it became an evil deed that Gideon and his family did.

Beware that in your plenty you don't forget the Lord your God and begin to disobey him.

TODAY _____

_____

_____

Colossians 3:5.   Judges 8:23, 24, 25, 27.   Deuteronomy 8:11.

**Don't be selfish,
don't live to make
a good impression
on others.
Be humble,
thinking of others
as better than yourself.**

When the Holy Spirit controls
our lives he will produce this
kind of fruit in us:
    love
      joy
        peace
          patience
            kindness
              goodness
                faithfulness
                  gentleness
                    and
                      self-control.
Give him first place in your life
and live as he wants you to.
Then we won't need to look for
honors and popularity, which
lead to jealousy and hard feelings.

TODAY _____

_____

_____

Philippians 2:3. Galatians 5:22, 23. Matthew 6:33. Galatians 5:26.

**Keep away
from anything
that might take
God's place
in your hearts.**

God wants us to turn from
godless living and sinful
pleasures and to live good,
God-fearing lives day after day.

Don't hide your light! Let it shine
for all; let your good deeds glow
for all to see, so that they will
praise your heavenly Father.

When he comes we will be like
him, as a result of seeing him as
he really is. And everyone who
really believes this will try to stay
pure because Christ is pure.

TODAY _____

_____

_____

1 John 5:21. Titus 2:12. Matthew 5:15, 16. 1 John 3:2, 3.

APRIL

1

**If you want
to know
what God wants
you to do,
ask him,
and he will
gladly tell you.**

He is always ready to give a bountiful supply of wisdom to all who ask him; he will not resent it. But when you ask him, be sure that you really expect him to tell you, for a doubtful mind will be as unsettled as a wave of the sea that is driven and tossed by the wind.

Trust the Lord completely; don't ever trust yourself. In everything you do, put God first, and he will direct you and crown your efforts with success.

He alone is God, and full of wisdom. Don't be conceited, sure of your own wisdom. Instead, trust and reverence the Lord.

_____**TODAY**

_____

_____

James 1:5a.   James 1:5b, 6.   Proverbs 3:5, 6.   1 Timothy 1:17.   Proverbs 3:7, 8.

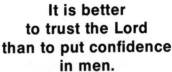

It is better
to trust the Lord
than to put confidence
in men.

King Asa sent his troops to meet them there. "O Lord," he cried out to God, "no one else can help us! Here we are, powerless against this mighty army. Oh, help us, Lord our God! For we trust in you alone to rescue us, and in your name we attack this vast horde. Don't let mere men defeat you!" Then the Lord defeated the Ethiopians, and Asa and the army of Judah triumphed as the Ethiopians fled.

Oh, praise the Lord, for he has listened to my pleadings! He is my strength, my shield from every danger. I trusted in him, and he helped me. The Lord protects his people.

TODAY _____

_____

_____

Psalm 118:8.   2 Chronicles 14:10, 11, 12.   Psalm 28:6, 7, 8.

What a wonderful God we have!

How great are his wisdom and knowledge and riches! How impossible it is for us to understand his decisions and his methods! For who among us can know the mind of the Lord? Who knows enough to be his counselor and guide?

And who could ever offer to the Lord enough to induce him to act? For everything comes from God alone. Everything lives by his power, and everything is for his glory. To him be glory evermore.

Give your bodies to God. Let them be a living sacrifice, holy—the kind he can accept. When you think of what he has done for you, is this too much to ask?

TODAY _____

_____

_____

Romans 11:33a.   Romans 11:33b, 34, 35, 36.   Romans 12:1.

Fight on for God.

"Don't worry about a thing,"
David told [Saul]. "I'll take care of
this Philistine!"

He picked up five smooth stones
from a stream and put them in his
shepherd's bag and, armed only with
his shepherd's staff and sling, started
across to Goliath.

Goliath walked out towards David
with his shield bearer ahead of
him, sneering in contempt.

David shouted in reply, "You come
to me with a sword and a spear,
but I come to you in the name

of the Lord of the armies of heaven
and of Israel—the very God
whom you have defied. . . .
The Lord does not depend on weapons
to fulfill his plans — he works
without regard to human means!''
    So David conquered the Philistine
giant with a sling and a stone.
    Our . . . power and success
comes from God.

TODAY _____

_____

1 Timothy 6:12.   1 Samuel 17:32, 40, 41, 45, 47, 50.   2 Corinthians 3:5.

APRIL

5

Problems and trials . . .
are good for us.

We are able to hold our heads
high no matter what happens
and know that all is well, for we
know how dearly God loves us.

Let God train you, for he is
doing what any loving father
does for his children. Whoever
heard of a son who was never
corrected? If God doesn't punish
you when you need it, as other
fathers punish their sons, then it
means that you aren't really
God's son at all—that you don't
really belong in his family. Being
punished isn't enjoyable while it is
happening—it hurts! But
afterwards we can see the result, a
quiet growth in grace and
character.

Go on growing in the Lord,
and become strong and vigorous in
the truth.

TODAY _____

_____

_____

Romans 5:3. Romans 5:5. Hebrews 12:7, 8, 11. Colossians 2:7.

**I will
not be
afraid.**

God carefully watches the goings
on of all mankind; he sees them
all. No darkness is thick enough to
hide evil men from his eyes.

You don't need to be afraid of
the dark any more, nor fear the
dangers of the day; nor dread the
plagues of darkness, nor
disasters in the morning.

Jehovah himself is caring for
you! He protects you day and
night. He keeps you from all evil,
and preserves your life.

TODAY _____

_____

_____

Psalm 23:4.   Job 34:21, 22.   Psalm 91:5, 6.   Psalm 121:5, 6.

**In the last days
it is going to be
very difficult
to be a Christian.**

For people will love only
themselves and their money; they
will be proud and boastful,
sneering at God, disobedient to
their parents, ungrateful to them,
and thoroughly bad. They will be
hardheaded and never give in to
others; they will be constant liars
and troublemakers and will think
nothing of immorality. They will
be rough and cruel, and sneer at
those who try to be good. They
will betray their friends; they will
be hotheaded, puffed up with
pride, and prefer good times to
worshiping God. They will go to
church, yes, but they won't really
believe anything they hear. Don't
be taken in by people like that.

You must keep on believing
the things you have been taught.

_____ **TODAY**

_____

_____

2 Timothy 3:1. 2 Timothy 3:2, 3, 4, 5, 14.

Which is the most important command?

Jesus replied, " 'Love the Lord your God with all your heart, soul, and mind.' This is the first and greatest commandment. The second most important is similar: 'Love your neighbor as much as you love yourself.' All the other commandments and all the demands of the prophets stem from these two laws and are fulfilled if you obey them. Keep only these and you will find that you are obeying all the others."

TODAY _____

_____

_____

Matthew 22:36. Matthew 22:37, 38, 39, 40.

APRIL

What is causing the quarrels and fights among you?

Isn't it because there is a whole army of evil desires within you?

You long for what others have . . . so you start a fight to take it away from them.

To quarrel with a neighbor is foolish; a man with good sense holds his tongue.

The tongue is a small thing, but what enormous damage it can do.

Don't criticize and speak evil about each other, dear brothers. If you do, you will be fighting against God's law of loving one another.

Give yourselves humbly to God. Resist the devil and he will flee from you.

TODAY _____

_____

_____

James 4:1. James 4:2. Proverbs 11:12. James 3:5. James 4:11, 7.

Get some sense and quit your sinning.

Turn from your sins . . . Put them behind you and receive a new heart and a new spirit.

Use every piece of God's armor to resist the enemy whenever he attacks, and when it is all over, you will still be standing up.

Get rid of all that is wrong in your life, both inside and outside, and humbly be glad for the wonderful message we have received, for it is able to save our souls as it takes hold of our hearts.

TODAY _____

_____

_____

1 Corinthians 15:34. Ezekiel 18:30, 31. Ephesians 6:13. James 1:21.

He [Jesus] died once for all to end sin's power.

God showed his great love for us by sending Christ to die for us while we were still sinners.

He personally carried the load of our sins in his own body when he died on the cross, so that we can be finished with sin and live a good life from now on.

He was oppressed and he was afflicted, yet he never said a word. He was brought as a lamb to the slaughter; and as a sheep before her shearers is dumb, so he stood silent before the ones condemning him. From prison and trial they led him away to his death.

Since Christ suffered and underwent pain, you must have the same attitude he did; you must be ready to suffer, too.

TODAY _____

_____

_____

Romans 6:10. Romans 5:8. 1 Peter 2:24. Isaiah 53:7, 8. 1 Peter 4:1.

Pilate laid open Jesus' back with a leaded whip.

And the soldiers made a crown of thorns and placed it on his head and robed him in royal purple. "Hail, 'King of the Jews!' " they mocked, and struck him with their fists.

At sight of him the chief priests and Jewish officials began yelling, "Crucify! Crucify!"

He was wounded and bruised for *our* sins. He was chastised that we might have peace; he was lashed—and we were healed! God laid on *him* the guilt and sins of every one of us!

_____ **TODAY**

_____

_____

John 19:1a.   John 19:1b, 2, 3, 6.   Isaiah 53:5, 6.

It was about nine o'clock in the morning when the crucifixion took place.

The people jeered at him as they walked by, and wagged their heads in mockery.

The chief priests and religious leaders were also standing around joking about Jesus.

And even the two robbers dying with him, cursed him.

Then Jesus called out with a loud voice, "Eli, Eli, lama sabachthani?" ("My God, my God, why have you deserted me?")

Then Jesus uttered another loud cry, and dismissed his spirit.

When the Roman officer standing beside his cross saw how he dismissed his spirit, he exclaimed, "Truly, this was the Son of God!"

TODAY _____

_____

_____

Mark 15:25. Mark 15:29, 31, 32, 34, 37, 39.

APRIL 14

"You say HE rose

**The First and Last,
the Living One who died,
who is now alive forevermore.**

As the new day was dawning, Mary
Magdalene and the other Mary
went out to the tomb.
Suddenly there was a great
earthquake; for an angel of the Lord
came down from heaven. . .
The angel spoke to the women.
"Don't be frightened!" he said.
"I know you are looking for Jesus,

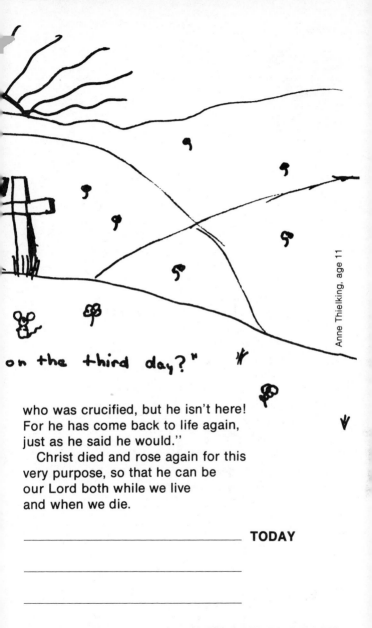

on the third day?"

who was crucified, but he isn't here!
For he has come back to life again,
just as he said he would."

Christ died and rose again for this
very purpose, so that he can be
our Lord both while we live
and when we die.

_____ **TODAY**

_____

_____

Revelation 1:18.   Matthew 28:1, 2, 5, 6.   Romans 14:9.

Keep me far from every wrong.

Show me the path where I should go, O Lord; point out the right road for me to walk. Lead me; teach me; for you are the God who gives me salvation. I have no hope except in you. Overlook my youthful sins, O Lord! Look at me instead through eyes of mercy and forgiveness, through eyes of everlasting love and kindness.

The Lord is good and glad to teach the proper path to all who go astray; he will teach the ways that are right and best to those who humbly turn to him. And when we obey him, every path he guides us on is fragrant with his lovingkindness and his truth.

TODAY _____

_____

_____

Psalm 119:29. Psalm 25:4, 5, 6, 7, 8, 9, 10.

God is my helper.
He is a friend of mine.

He is for me! How can I be afraid? What can mere man do to me?

My health fails; my spirits droop, yet God remains! He is the strength of my heart; he is mine forever!

The Lord is good. When trouble comes, he is the place to go! And he knows everyone who trusts in him!

I get as close to him as I can! I have chosen him and I will tell everyone about the wonderful ways he rescues me.

_____ **TODAY**

_____

_____

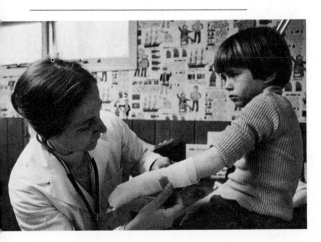

Psalm 54:4.   Psalm 118:6.   Psalm 73:26.   Nahum 1:7.   Psalm 73:28.

APRIL

17

Usually no one will hurt you for wanting to do good.

But even if they should, you are to be envied, for God will reward you for it. Quietly trust yourself to Christ your Lord and if anybody asks why you believe as you do, be ready to tell him, and do it in a gentle and respectful way.

Do what is right; then if men speak against you, calling you evil names, they will become ashamed of themselves for falsely accusing you when you have only done what is good. Remember, if God wants you to suffer, it is better to suffer for doing good than for doing wrong!

Christ also suffered. He died. . . that he might bring us safely home to God.

TODAY _____

_____

1 Peter 3:13.   1 Peter 3:14, 15, 16, 17, 18.

Give your parents joy!

Don't let anyone think little of
you because you are young. Be
their ideal; let them follow the way
you teach and live; be a pattern
for them in your love, your faith,
and your clean thoughts.

It's wonderful to be young! Enjoy
every minute of it! Do all you
want to; take in everything, but
realize that you must account to
God for everything you do.

So banish grief and pain, but
remember that youth, with a whole
life before it, can make serious
mistakes.

_____ **TODAY**

_____

_____

Proverbs 23:25.   1 Timothy 4:12.   Ecclesiastes 11:9, 10.

I will not abandon you.

Caleb reassured the people as they stood before Moses. "Let us go up at once and possess it," he said, "for we are well able to conquer it!"

"Not against people as strong as they are!" the other spies said. "They would crush us!"

When I am afraid, I will put my confidence in you. Yes, I will trust the promises of God. And since I am trusting him, what can mere man do to me? The very day I call for help, the tide of battle turns. My enemies flee! This one thing I *know: God is for me!*

TODAY _____

_____

_____

John 14:18. Numbers 13:30, 31. Psalm 56:3, 4, 9.

**You will keep on
guiding me all my life
with your wisdom and counsel;
and afterwards receive me
into the glories of heaven!**

No one can hold back his spirit
from departing; no one has the
power to prevent his day of death.

We know that when this tent
we live in now is taken
down—when we die and leave
these bodies—we will have
wonderful new bodies in heaven,
homes that will be ours
forevermore, made for us by God
himself.

And we are not afraid, but are
quite content to die, for then we
will be at home with the Lord.

_____ **TODAY**

_____

_____

Psalm 73:24.   Ecclesiastes 8:8.   2 Corinthians 5:1, 8.

Come, Lord Jesus!

There are many homes up there where my Father lives, and I am going to prepare them for your coming. When everything is ready, then I will come and get you, so that you can always be with me where I am.

Men of faith . . . saw it all awaiting them on ahead and were glad, for they agreed that this earth was not their real home but that they were just strangers visiting down here. And quite obviously when they talked like that, they were looking forward to their real home in heaven.

We who are still alive and remain on the earth will be caught up with them in the clouds to meet the Lord in the air and remain with him forever.

TODAY _____

_____

_____

Revelation 22:20. John 14:2, 3. Hebrews 11:13, 14. 1 Thessalonians 4:17.

**God will judge us
for everything we do;
including every
hidden thing,
good or bad.**

I [God] don't make decisions the
way you do! Men judge by
outward appearance, but I look at
a man's thoughts and intentions.

Let men cast off their wicked
deeds; let them banish from their
minds the very thought of doing
wrong! Let them turn to the Lord
that he may have mercy upon
them, and to our God, for he
will abundantly pardon!

His joy is in those who
reverence him, those who expect
him to be loving and kind.

TODAY _____

_____

_____

_____

Ecclesiastes 12:14. 1 Samuel 16:7. Isaiah 55:7. Psalm 147:11.

Am I a God who is only in one place?

Can anyone hide from me? Am I not everywhere in all of heaven and earth?

O Lord . . . You know when I sit or stand. When far away you know my every thought. You chart the path ahead of me, and tell me where to stop and rest. Every moment, you know where I am. You know what I am going to say before I even say it.

He knows about everyone, everywhere. Everything about us is bare and wide open to the all-seeing eyes of our living God; nothing can be hidden from him to whom we must explain all that we have done.

TODAY _____

_____

_____

Jeremiah 23:23, 24. Psalm 139:1, 2, 3, 4. Hebrews 4:13.

I am closely watching you and I see every sin.

No amount of soap or lye can make you clean. You are stained with guilt that cannot ever be washed away. I see it always before me, the Lord God says.

Yet now God declares us "not guilty" of offending him if we trust in Jesus Christ, who in his kindness freely takes away our sins.

For God sent Christ Jesus to take the punishment for our sins and to end all God's anger against us.

_____ **TODAY**

_____

_____

Jeremiah 16:17.   Jeremiah 2:22.   Romans 3:24, 25.

APRIL

25

**Before
anything else
existed,
there was
Christ.**

He created everything there is—
nothing exists that he didn't make.

But although he made the
world, the world didn't recognize
him when he came. Even in his
own land and among his own
people, the Jews, he was not
accepted. Only a few would
welcome and receive him. But to
all who received him, he gave the
right to become children of God.
All they needed to do was to trust
him to save them.

TODAY

John 1:1.   John 1:3, 10, 11, 12.

He spoke, and they were healed— snatched from the door of death.

When Jesus arrived in Capernaum, a Roman army captain came and pled with him to come to his home and heal his servant boy who was in bed paralyzed and racked with pain.

"Yes," Jesus said, "I will come and heal him."

Then the officer said, "Sir, I am not worthy to have you in my home; [and it isn't necessary for you to come]. If you will only stand here and say, 'Be healed,' my servant will get well! I know, because I am under the authority of my superior officers and I have authority over my soldiers, and I say to one, 'Go,' and he goes, and to another, 'Come,' and he comes, and to my slave boy, 'Do this or that,' and he does it. And I know you have authority to tell his sickness to go—and it will go!"

Jesus stood there amazed! Turning to the crowd he said, "I haven't seen faith like this in all the land of Israel!"

God. . . is able to do far more than we would ever dare to ask or even dream of.

TODAY _____

_____

Psalm 107:20.   Matthew 8:5, 6, 7, 8, 9, 10.   Ephesians 3:20.

As long as
the earth remains,
there will be . . .
day and night.

Have you ever once commanded the morning to appear, and caused the dawn to rise in the east?

Have you ever told the daylight to spread to the ends of the earth?

Have you ever robed the dawn in red?

Tell me about the darkness. Where does it come from? Can you find its boundaries, or go to its source?

God said, "Let there be light." And light appeared . . . So he let it shine for awhile, and then there was darkness again . . . Together they formed the first day.

TODAY _____

_____

_____

Genesis 8:22. Job 38:12, 13, 14, 19, 20. Genesis 1:3, 4, 5.

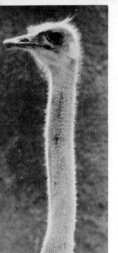

O Lord, what a variety you have made!

He sends the night and darkness, when all the forest folk come out. Then the young lions roar for their food, but they are dependent on the Lord. At dawn they slink back into their dens to rest, and men go off to work until the evening shadows fall again.

Before me lies the mighty ocean, teeming with life of every kind, both great and small. And look! See the ships! And over there, the whale you made to play in the sea.

In wisdom you have made them all! The earth is full of your riches.

TODAY _____

_____

_____

Psalm 104:24a.   Psalm 104:20, 21, 22, 23, 25, 24b.

APRIL

**Show me
your strong love
in wonderful ways,
O Savior of all those
seeking your help
against their foes.**

Moses told the people, "Don't be afraid. Just stand where you are and watch, and you will see the wonderful way the Lord will rescue you today."

Moses stretched his rod over the sea, and the Lord opened up a path through the sea, with walls of water on each side. So the people of Israel walked through the sea on dry ground! Then the Egyptians followed them between the walls of water along the bottom of the sea. When all the Israelites were on the other side. . . the sea returned to normal beneath the morning light. The Egyptians tried to flee, but the Lord drowned them in the sea.

His never-failing love protects.

TODAY _____

_____

_____

Psalm 17:7.   Exodus 14:13, 21, 22, 23, 26, 27.   Psalm 31:21.

I will never, *never* fail you nor forsake you.

I will not abandon you or leave you as orphans in the storm—I will come to you.

I am with you always, even to the end of the world. I am the First and Last, the Living One who died, who is now alive forevermore.

That is why we can say without any doubt or fear, "The Lord is my Helper and I am not afraid of anything that mere man can do to me."

If my father and mother should abandon me, [God] would welcome and comfort me.

TODAY _____

_____

_____

Hebrews 13:5. John 14:18. Matthew 28:20. Revelation 1:18. Hebrews 13:6. Psalm 27:10.

MAY

Jesus shouted, "Father, I commit my spirit to you," and with those words he died.

From prison and trial they led him away to his death. But who among the people of that day realized it was their sins that he was dying for—that he was suffering their punishment? He was buried like a criminal in a rich man's grave; but he had done no wrong, and had never spoken an evil word.

Yet it was the Lord's good plan to bruise him and fill him with grief . . . He shall live again and God's program shall prosper in his hands.

TODAY _____

_____

_____

Luke 23:46. Isaiah 53:8, 9, 10.

Be anxious to do the will of God.

Since Christ suffered and underwent pain, you must have the same attitude he did; you must be ready to suffer, too.

And you won't be spending the rest of your life chasing after evil desires, but will be anxious to do the will of God.

Of course, your former friends will be very surprised when you don't eagerly join them any more in the wicked things they do, and they will laugh at you in contempt and scorn.

But just remember that they must face the Judge of all, living and dead; they will be punished for the way they have lived.

_____ **TODAY**

_____

_____

1 Peter 4:2.   1 Peter 4:1, 2, 4, 5.

MAY 3

**God did not
send his Son
into the world
to condemn it,
but to save it.**

For unto us a Child is born;
unto us a Son is given; and the
government shall be upon his
shoulder. These will be his royal
titles:

WONDERFUL
COUNSELOR
THE MIGHTY GOD
THE EVERLASTING FATHER
THE PRINCE OF PEACE

His ever-expanding, peaceful
government will never end. . .
He will bring true justice and peace
to all the nations of the world.

TODAY _____

_____

_____

John 3:17. Isaiah 9:6, 7.

Patty Vanderveld, age 9

The Lord is coming soon.

[The Lord] isn't really being slow
about his promised return . . .
He is waiting, for the good reason
that he is not willing that any
should perish, and he is giving
more time for sinners to repent.

We are looking forward to God's
promise of new heavens and a
new earth afterwards, where there
will be only goodness.

While you are waiting for these
things to happen and for him to
come, try hard to live without
sinning; and be at peace with
everyone so that he will be pleased
with you when he returns.

TODAY _____

_____

_____

Philippians 4:5. 2 Peter 3:9, 13, 14.

MAY

Keep away from every kind of evil. Be happy if you are cursed and insulted for being a Christian.

In everything you do, stay away from complaining and arguing, so that no one can speak a word of blame against you. You are to live clean, innocent lives as children of God in a dark world full of people who are crooked and stubborn. Shine out among them like beacon lights.

Live as Christians should.

Never forget to be truthful and kind. Hold these virtues tightly. Write them deep within your heart.

TODAY _____

_____

Philippians 1:27. 1 Thessalonians 5:22. 1 Peter 4:14. Philippians 2:14,15. Proverbs 3:3, 4.

Rodney Schlenker, age 9

Your words are a flashlight to light the path ahead of me.

I [Jesus] have come as a Light to shine in this dark world, so that all who put their trust in me will no longer wander in the darkness.

Though once your heart was full of darkness, now it is full of light from the Lord, and your behavior should show it! Because of this light within you, you should do only what is good and right and true. Learn as you go along what pleases the Lord.

Love comes from God and those who are loving and kind show that they are the children of God, and that they are getting to know him better. But if a person isn't loving and kind, it shows that he doesn't know God—for God is love.

TODAY _____

_____

_____

Psalm 119:105. John 12:46. Ephesians 5:8, 9, 10. 1 John 4:7, 8.

To learn,
you must want
to be taught.

How does a man become wise?
The first step is to trust and
reverence the Lord!

Only fools refuse to be taught.
Listen to your father and mother.
What you learn from them will
stand you in good stead; it will
gain you many honors.

You must keep on believing the
things you have been taught . . .
It is these that make you wise to
accept God's salvation by
trusting in Christ Jesus.

TODAY _____

_____

_____

Proverbs 12:1.   Proverbs 1:7, 8, 9.   2 Timothy 3:14, 15.

Happy are all who perfectly follow the laws of God.

You know how, when you were a small child, you were taught the holy Scriptures; and it is these that make you wise to accept God's salvation by trusting in Christ Jesus.

The whole Bible was given to us by inspiration from God and is useful to teach us what is true and to make us realize what is wrong in our lives; it straightens us out and helps us do what is right. It is God's way of making us well prepared at every point, fully equipped to do good to everyone.

_____ **TODAY**

_____

_____

Psalm 119:1.   2 Timothy 3:15, 16, 17.

Check up on yourselves.
Are you really Christians?

Do you pass the test? Do you feel Christ's presence and power more and more within you? Or are you just pretending to be Christians when actually you aren't at all?

Someone may say, "I am a Christian; I am on my way to heaven; I belong to Christ." But if he doesn't do what Christ tells him to, he is a liar. But those who do what Christ tells them to will learn to love God more and more. That is the way to know whether or not you are a Christian. Anyone who says he is a Christian should live as Christ did.

TODAY _____

_____

_____

2 Corinthians 13:5a.   2 Corinthians 13:5b.   1 John 2:4, 5, 6.

MAY

Eagles have been seen flying beside high-flying airplanes. They live high as well—building their huge nests of sticks high in the mountains or in very tall trees. Eagles return each year to the same nest, repairing and adding to its weight until it may weigh as much as a ton. Eventually the weight kills the tree—and the whole mass crashes to the ground.

Whatever you do or say, let it be as a representative of the Lord Jesus.

Work hard and cheerfully at all you do, just as though you were working for the Lord and not merely for your masters, remembering that it is the Lord Christ who is going to pay you, giving you your full portion of all he owns. He is the one you are really working for.

And if you don't do your best for him, he will pay you in a way that you won't like—for he has no special favorites who can get away with shirking.

TODAY _____

_____

_____

Colossians 3:17. Colossians 3:23, 24, 25.

Pride disgusts the Lord.
Take my word for it—
proud men shall be punished.

Proud men end in shame.
Claiming themselves to be wise
without God, they became utter
fools instead.

So be careful. If you are thinking,
"Oh, I would never behave like
that"—let this be a warning to you.
For you too may fall into sin.

Though you soar as high as
eagles, and build your nest
among the stars, I will bring you
plummeting down, says the Lord.

TODAY _____

_____

_____

Proverbs 16:5. Proverbs 11:2. Romans 1:22. 1 Corinthians 10:12. Obadiah 4.

12

The Lord is very great, and lives in heaven.

He is high above the nations; his glory is far greater than the heavens. Far below him are the heavens and the earth; he stoops to look, and lifts the poor from the dirt, and the hungry from the garbage dump, and sets them among princes.

His compassion never ends. His lovingkindness begins afresh each day.

TODAY _____

_____

_____

_____

Isaiah 33:5.   Psalm 113:4, 6, 7, 8.   Lamentations 3:22, 23.

MAY

**Everyone
who calls upon
the name of the Lord
will be saved.**

Salvation that comes from trusting
Christ. . . is already within easy
reach of us; in fact, it is as near
as our own hearts and mouths.

For if you tell others with your
own mouth that Jesus Christ is
your Lord, and believe in your
own heart that God has raised him
from the dead, you will be saved.
For it is by believing in his heart
that a man becomes right with
God; and with his mouth he tells
others of his faith, confirming his
salvation. For the Scriptures tell us
that no one who believes in
Christ will ever be disappointed.

TODAY_____

_____

Joel 2:32. Romans 10:8, 9, 10, 11.

**God will . . . make you
as good as you wish
you could be!**

For God is at work within you,
helping you want to obey him,
and then helping you do what he
wants.

Do not resent it when God
chastens and corrects you, for
his punishment is proof of his love.
Just as a father punishes a son
he delights in to make him better,
so the Lord corrects you.

Then everyone will be praising
the name of the Lord Jesus
Christ because of the results they
see in you; and your greatest
glory will be that you belong to
him.

TODAY _____

_____

2 Thessalonians 1:11. Philippians 2:13. Proverbs 3:11, 12. 2 Thessalonians 1:12.

MAY 15

**O Lord our God,
the majesty and glory
of your name
fills all the earth
and overflows
the heavens.**

You have taught the little
children to praise you perfectly.
May their example shame and
silence your enemies.

O Lord, I will praise you with
all my heart, and tell everyone
about the marvelous things you
do.

Turn us again to yourself, O
God of the armies of heaven.
Look down on us, your face
aglow with joy and love — only
then shall we be saved.

_____ **TODAY**

_____

_____

Psalm 8:1. Psalm 8:2. Psalm 9:1. Psalm 80:19.

Turn me again to you
and restore me,
for you alone
are the Lord,
my God.

I turned away from God but I was sorry afterwards. I kicked myself for my stupidity.

The Lord still waits for you to come to him, so he can show you his love.

If you leave God's paths and go astray, you will hear a Voice behind you say, "No, this is the way; walk here."

For he holds our lives in his hands. And he holds our feet to the path.

TODAY _____

_____

_____

Jeremiah 31:18, 19.   Isaiah 30:18, 21.   Psalm 66:9.

**Everything we have
has come from you.**

Food and drink . . . even this pleasure is from the hand of God. For who can eat or enjoy apart from him?

He sends rain upon the mountains and fills the earth with fruit. The tender grass grows up at his command to feed the cattle, and there are fruit trees, vegetables and grain for man to cultivate.

He gives food to every living thing, for his lovingkindness continues forever. Oh, give thanks to the God of heaven.

TODAY_____

_____

_____

1 Chronicles 29:14. Ecclesiastes 2:24, 25. Psalm 104:13, 14. Psalm 136:25, 26.

18

It is good to say, "Thank you" to the Lord.

Every morning tell him, "Thank you for your kindness," and every evening rejoice in all his faithfulness.

Come before him with thankful hearts.

For the Lord is a great God, the great King of all gods. He controls the formation of the depths of the earth and the mightiest mountains; all are his. He made the sea and formed the land; they too are his.

He is our God. We are his sheep and he is our Shepherd.

TODAY _____

_____

_____

Psalm 92:1.   Psalm 92:2.   Psalm 95:2, 3, 4, 5, 7.

You are the Ruler of all mankind; your hand controls power and might.

David shouted in reply, "You come to me with a sword and a spear, but I come to you in the name of the Lord of the armies of heaven and of Israel—the very God whom you have defied." David . . . reaching into his shepherd's bag, took out a stone, hurled it from his sling, and hit the Philistine in the forehead. The stone sank in, and the man fell on his face to the ground. So David conquered the Philistine giant with a sling and a stone.

The best-equipped army cannot save a king—for great strength is not enough to save anyone. But the eyes of the Lord are watching over those who fear him, who rely upon his steady love.

_____ **TODAY**

_____

_____

1 Chronicles 29:12.   1 Samuel 17:45, 49, 50.   Psalm 33:16, 18.

MAY

20

**The reason
you don't have
what you want
is that you don't
ask God for it.**

Ask, and you will be given what
you ask for. Seek, and you will
find. Knock, and the door will be
opened. For everyone who asks,
receives. Anyone who seeks, finds.
If only you will knock, the door
will open.

And we are sure of this, that
he will listen to us whenever we
ask him for anything in line with
his will. And if we really know he
is listening when we talk to him
and make our requests, then we
can be sure that he will answer us.

TODAY _____

_____

_____

James 4:2.   Matthew 7:7, 8.   1 John 5:14, 15.

Tell me what to do, O Lord.

What does the Lord your God require of you except to listen carefully to all he says to you, and to obey for your own good the commandments I am giving you today, and to love him, and to worship him with all your hearts and souls?

He will keep in perfect peace all those who trust in him, whose thoughts turn often to the Lord! Trust in the Lord God always, for in the Lord Jehovah is your everlasting strength.

For good men the path is not uphill and rough! God does not give them a rough and treacherous path, but smooths the road before them.

TODAY _____

_____

_____

Psalm 27:11.   Deuteronomy 10:12, 13.   Isaiah 26:3, 4, 7.

22

Cast off and throw away all these rotten garments of anger, hatred, cursing, and dirty language.

Don't tell lies to each other; it was your old life with all its wickedness that did that sort of thing; now it is dead and gone.

You are living a brand new kind of
life that is continually learning
more and more of what is right,
and trying constantly to be more
and more like Christ who created
this new life within you. In this
new life one's nationality or race or
education or social position is
unimportant; such things mean
nothing. Whether a person has
Christ is what matters, and he is
equally available to all.

_____ **TODAY**

_____

_____

Colossians 3:8.   Colossians 3:9, 10, 11.

The Lord despises the deeds of the wicked, but loves those who try to be good.

The Lord says, "The people . . . have sinned again and again, and I will not forget it."

"I will make you groan as a wagon groans that is loaded with sheaves. Your swiftest warriors will stumble in flight. The strong will all be weak, and the great ones can no longer save themselves. The archer's aim will fail, the swiftest runners won't be fast enough to flee, and even the best of horsemen can't outrun the danger then. The most courageous of your mighty men will drop their weapons and run for their lives that day." The Lord God has spoken.

God has come in this way to show you his awesome power, so that from now on you will be afraid to sin against him!

TODAY _____

_____

_____

Proverbs 15:9.   Amos 1:3.   Amos 2:13, 14, 15, 16.   Exodus 20:20.

MAY

24

The Lord stands up! He is the great Prosecuting Attorney presenting his case against his people!

God will judge us for everything we do, including every hidden thing, good or bad.

Lord, if you keep in mind our sins then who can ever get an answer to his prayers? But you forgive! What an awesome thing this is!

He has not punished us as we deserve for all our sins, for his mercy toward those who fear and honor him is as great as the height of the heavens above the earth.

TODAY _____

_____

Isaiah 3:13. Ecclesiastes 12:14. Psalm 130:3, 4. Psalm 103:10, 11.

**Don't act
like the people
who make horoscopes
and try to read
their fate and future
in the stars!**

Don't be frightened by
predictions such as theirs, for it
is all a pack of lies. Their ways are
futile and foolish. They cut down
a tree and carve an idol, and
decorate it with gold and silver
and fasten it securely in place with
hammer and nails, so that it
won't fall over, and there stands
their god like a helpless
scarecrow in a garden!

   O Lord, there is no other god
like you. For you are great and
your name is full of power.

TODAY _____

_____

_____

Jeremiah 10:2.   Jeremiah 10:3, 4, 5, 6.

Sing to the Lord!

Great and marvelous
Are your doings,
Lord God Almighty.
Just and true
Are your ways,
O King of Ages.
Who shall not fear,
O Lord,
And glorify your Name?
For you alone are holy.

TODAY _____

_____

_____

Psalm 95:1. Revelation 15:3, 4.

Holy, holy, holy
is the Lord of Hosts.

Even the heavens can't be absolutely pure compared with him!

The moon and stars are less than nothing as compared to him.

Who else is like the Lord among the gods? Who is glorious in holiness like him?

Be holy now in everything you do, just as the Lord is holy, who invited you to be his child.

Try hard to live without sinning; and be at peace with everyone so that he will be pleased with you when he returns.

_____ **TODAY**

_____

_____

Isaiah 6:3. Job 15:15. Job 25:5. Exodus 15:11. 1 Peter 1:15. 2 Peter 3:14.

**The Lord knows
what you have done.**

He will judge your deeds.

Don't be misled; remember that you can't ignore God and get away with it: a man will always reap just the kind of crop he sows! If he sows to please his own wrong desires, he will be planting seeds of evil and he will surely reap a harvest of spiritual decay and death.

What profit is there if you gain the whole world—and lose eternal life? What can be compared with the value of eternal life?

_____ **TODAY**

_____

_____

1 Samuel 2:3.   Galatians 6:7, 8.   Matthew 16:26.

Though tiny, ants know how to get things done. Picture a man carrying a Volkswagen—and you have some idea of the load ants carry when gathering food for the winter.

Don't copy the behavior and customs of this world.

Don't be teamed with those who do not love the Lord, for what do the people of God have in common with the people of sin? How can light live with darkness? And what harmony can there be between Christ and the devil? How can a Christian be a partner with one who doesn't believe?

Stop loving this evil world and all that it offers you, for when you love these things you show that you do not really love God.

Be a new and different person with a fresh newness in all you do and think.

TODAY _____

_____

_____

Romans 12:2a.   2 Corinthians 6:14, 15.   1 John 2:15.   Romans 12:2b.

Whatever you do, do well.

Take a lesson from the ants.

They aren't strong, but store up food for the winter.

Learn from their ways and be wise! For though they have no king to make them work, yet they labor hard all summer, gathering food for the winter.

Tackle every task that comes along, and if you fear God you can expect his blessing.

Hard work means prosperity; only a fool idles away his time.

TODAY _____

_____

_____

Ecclesiastes 9:10. Proverbs 6:6. Proverbs 30:24. Proverbs 6:6, 7, 8. Ecclesiastes 7:18. Proverbs 12:11.

Don't hide your light!
Let it shine for all.

Feed the hungry! Help those in
trouble! Then your light will
shine out from the darkness, and
the darkness around you shall be
as bright as day.

Bring right into your own
homes those who are helpless,
poor and destitute. Clothe those
who are cold and don't hide from
relatives who need your help.

You are the world's light—a city
on a hill, glowing in the night
for all to see . . . so that they will
praise your heavenly Father.

_____

_____

_____

Matthew 5:15, 16.   Isaiah 58:10, 7.   Matthew 5:14, 16.

Practice loving each other.

I am not writing out a new rule for you to obey, for it is an old one you have always had, right from the start. You have heard it all before.

Yet it is always new, and works for you just as it did for Christ; and as we obey this commandment, *to love one another,* the darkness in our lives disappears and the new light of life in Christ shines in.

For though once your heart was full of darkness, now it is full of light from the Lord, and your behavior should show it!

_____ **TODAY**

_____

_____

1 John 4:7.   1 John 2:7, 8.   Ephesians 5:8.

Love comes from God.

Those who are loving and kind
show that they are the children
of God, and that they are getting
to know him better. But if a
person isn't loving and kind, it
shows that he doesn't know
God—for God is love.

God showed how much he
loved us by sending his only Son
into this wicked world to bring
to us eternal life through his death.

Since God loved us as much
as that, we surely ought to love
each other too. For though we
have never yet seen God, when we
love each other God lives in us
and his love within us grows ever
stronger.

TODAY _____

_____

_____

1 John 4:7.   1 John 4:8, 9, 11, 12.

God
loved
the world.

He did not spare even his own
Son for us but gave him up for
us all.

Anyone who believes in him
shall . . . have eternal life.

There is salvation in no one
else! Under all heaven there is no
other name for men to call upon
to save them.

And he is able to keep you
from slipping and falling away, and
to bring you, sinless and perfect,
into his glorious presence with
mighty shouts of everlasting joy.
Amen.

TODAY _____

_____

_____

John 3:16. Romans 8:32. John 3:16. Acts 4:12. Jude 25.

**If anybody asks
why you believe as you do,
be ready to tell him.**

Do it in a gentle and respectful way.
For if you talk meekly and courteously to them they are more likely, with God's help, to turn away from their wrong ideas and believe what is true.
Be wise in all your contacts with them. Let your conversation be gracious as well as sensible, for then you will have the right answer for everyone.

TODAY _____

_____

_____

1 Peter 3:15.   2 Timothy 2:25.   Colossians 4:5, 6.

JUNE

5

Is anything too hard for God?

Commit everything you do to the Lord. Trust him to help you do it and he will.

Don't worry about anything; instead, pray about everything; tell God your needs and don't forget to thank him for his answers.

Let him have all your worries and cares, for he is always thinking about you and watching everything that concerns you.

Be delighted with the Lord. Then he will give you all your heart's desires.

TODAY _____

_____

_____

Genesis 18:14. Psalm 37:5. Philippians 4:6. 1 Peter 5:7. Psalm 37:4.

JUNE

The Lord is coming soon.

Let all the world look to me for
salvation! For I am God; there is
no other.

Every knee in all the world
shall bow to me, and every tongue
shall swear allegiance to my
name.

"In Jehovah is all my
righteousness and strength," the
people shall declare. And all who
were angry with him shall come to
him and be ashamed.

Yes, each of us will give an
account of himself to God.

TODAY _____

_____

_____

Philippians 4:5. Isaiah 45:22, 23, 24. Romans 14:12.

Let everyone be sure that he is doing his very best.

For then he will have the personal satisfaction of work well done, and won't need to compare himself with someone else.

If you wait for perfect conditions, you will never get anything done.

Keep on sowing your seed, for you never know which will grow—perhaps it all will.

It's wonderful to be young!
Enjoy every minute of it! Do all you
want to; take in everything, but
realize that you must account to
God for everything you do.

_____ **TODAY**

_____

_____

Galatians 6:4.   Ecclesiastes 11:4, 6, 9.

JUNE

**It is hard
to stop a quarrel
once it starts,
so don't let it begin.**

You should be like one big
happy family, full of sympathy
toward each other, loving one
another with tender hearts and
humble minds.

Don't repay evil for evil. Don't
snap back at those who say unkind
things about you. Instead, pray
for God's help for them, for we are
to be kind to others, and God
will bless us for it.

Be humble and gentle. Be
patient with each other, making
allowance for each other's faults
because of your love.

TODAY _____

_____

_____

Proverbs 17:14.   1 Peter 3:8, 9.   Ephesians 4:2.

**Dislike
of others
should have
no place
in your lives.**

So get rid of your feelings of hatred. Don't just pretend to be good! Be done with dishonesty and jealousy and talking about others behind their backs.

Throw away all these rotten garments of anger, hatred, cursing, and dirty language.

Dear brothers, I am not writing out a new rule for you to obey, for it is an old one you have always had, right from the start. You have heard it all before. Yet it is always new, and works for you just as it did for Christ; and as we obey this commandment, *to love one another,* the darkness in our lives disappears and the new light of life in Christ shines in.

TODAY _____

_____

_____

Ephesians 4:31.   1 Peter 2:1.   Colossians 3:8.   1 John 2:7, 8.

JUNE 10

He [God] is like a father to us, tender and sympathetic.

We are all children of God through faith in Jesus Christ. For all who are led by the Spirit of God are sons of God.

See how very much our heavenly Father loves us, for he allows us to be called his children—think of it—and we really *are!* But since most people don't know God, naturally they don't understand that we are his children. Yes, dear friends, we are already God's children, right now, and we can't even imagine what it is going to be like later on. But we do know this, that when he comes we will be like him, as a result of seeing him as he really is.

TODAY _____

_____

Psalm 103:13. Galatians 3:26. Romans 8:14. 1 John 3:1, 2.

I know the plans
I have for you,
says the Lord.

His unchanging plan has always been to adopt us into his own family by sending Jesus Christ to die for us.

It is he who saved us and chose us for his holy work, not because we deserved it but because that was his plan long before the world began.

You didn't choose me! I chose you! I appointed you to go and produce lovely fruit always.

When the Holy Spirit controls our lives he will produce this kind of fruit in us: love, joy, peace, patience, kindness, goodness, faithfulness, gentleness and self-control.

TODAY _____

_____

_____

Jeremiah 29:11. Ephesians 1:5. 2 Timothy 1:9. John 15:16. Galatians 5:22, 23.

JUNE

12

Jesus was led out into the wilderness by the Holy Spirit, to be tempted there by Satan.

Even though Jesus was God's Son, he had to learn from experience what it was like to obey, when obeying meant suffering.

The wrong desires that come into your life aren't anything new and different. Many others have faced exactly the same problems before you. And no temptation is irresistible. You can trust God to keep the temptation from becoming so strong that you can't stand up against it, for he has promised this and will do what he says.

TODAY _____

_____

_____

Matthew 4:1. Hebrews 5:8. 1 Corinthians 10:13.

JUNE 13

Just as a father punishes a son he delights in to make him better, so the Lord corrects you.

Do not resent it when God chastens and corrects you, for his punishment is proof of his love.

Let God train you, for he is doing what any loving father does for his children. Whoever heard of a son who was never corrected?

If God doesn't punish you when you need it, as other fathers punish their sons, then it means that you . . . don't really belong in his family.

Since we respect our fathers here on earth, though they punish us, should we not all the more cheerfully submit to God's training so that we can begin really to live?

_____ **TODAY**

_____

_____

Proverbs 3:12. Proverbs 3:11. Hebrews 12:7, 8, 9.

JUNE
14

When someone
becomes a Christian
he becomes a
brand new person
inside.
He is not
the same any more.
A new life
has begun!

Then it will be as though I had sprinkled clean water on you, for you will be clean. And I will give you a new heart—I will give you new and right desires—and put a new spirit within you. I will take out your stony hearts of sin and give you new hearts of love.

And I will put my Spirit within you so that you will obey my laws and do whatever I command.

TODAY

_____

_____

_____

2 Corinthians 5:17.   Ezekiel 36:25, 26, 27.

JUNE

15

Your strong love for each other will prove to the world that you are my disciples.

We know what real love is from Christ's example in dying for us.

Let us practice loving each other, for love comes from God and those who are loving and kind show that they are the children of God, and that they are getting to know him better.

And this is what God says we must do: Believe on the name of his Son Jesus Christ, and love one another.

TODAY _____

_____

John 13:35. 1 John 3:16. 1 John 4:7. 1 John 3:23.

**Follow God's example
in everything you do
just as a much loved child
imitates his father.**

He is good to everyone, and his
compassion is intertwined with
everything he does.

He saved us—not because we
were good enough to be saved, but
because of his kindness and pity.

Because of this light within you,
you should do only what is good
and right and true.

Love your enemies! Pray for
those who *persecute* you! In that
way you will be acting as true
sons of your Father in heaven.

TODAY _____

_____

Ephesians 5:1.   Psalm 145:9.   Titus 3:5.   Ephesians 5:9.   Matthew 5:44, 45.

JUNE
17

If young baboons quarrel with older baboons, they are kicked out of their tree and have to find another place to sleep.

Obey God because you are his children.

Don't slip back into your old ways—doing evil because you knew no better.

But be holy now in everything you do, just as the Lord is holy, who invited you to be his child. He himself has said, "You must be holy, for I am holy."

For you have a new life. It was not passed on to you from your parents, for the life they gave you will fade away. This new one will last forever, for it comes from Christ, God's ever-living Message to men.

And remember that your heavenly Father to whom you pray has no favorites when he judges. He will judge you with perfect justice for everything you do; so act in reverent fear of him from now on until you get to heaven.

TODAY _____

_____

_____

1 Peter 1:14a. 1 Peter 1:14b, 15, 16, 23, 17.

**I will try to walk
a blameless path,
but how I need
your help,
especially
in my own home,
where I long to act
as I should.**

In my mind I want to be
God's willing servant but
instead I find myself still
enslaved to sin.

So you see how it is:
my new life tells me to do right,
but the old nature that is still
inside me loves to sin.

Overwhelming victory is
ours through Christ who
loved us enough to die for
us.

Ask the Lord Jesus to help
you live as you should.

TODAY _____

_____

_____

Psalm 101:2. Romans 7:23, 24. Romans 8:37. Romans 13:14.

**Live by the principles
of love and justice,
and always be expecting
much from him,
your God.**

Happy are those who long
to be just and good, for
they shall be completely
satisfied.

Happy are the kind and
merciful, for they shall be
shown mercy.

Happy are those whose
hearts are pure, for they
shall see God.

Happy are those who strive
for peace—they shall be
called the sons of God.

TODAY _____

_____

_____

Hosea 12:6.   Matthew 5:6, 7, 8, 9.

JUNE

20

**Do only
what is good
and right
and true.**

If you have really heard his
[Christ's] voice and learned from
him the truths concerning himself,
then throw off your old evil
nature—the old you that was a
partner in your evil ways—rotten
through and through, full of lust
and sham.

Now your attitudes and thoughts
must all be constantly changing
for the better.

Yes, you must be a new and
different person, holy and good.
Clothe yourself with this new
nature.

TODAY _____

_____

_____

Ephesians 5:9.   Ephesians 4:21, 22, 23, 24.

You shall give due honor and respect to the elderly.

Anna, a prophetess . . . was very old, for she had been a widow for eighty-four years following seven years of marriage. She never left the Temple but stayed there night and day, worshiping God by praying and often fasting.

Care for widows who are poor and alone in the world, if they are looking to God for his help and spending much time in prayer.

Praise the Lord . . . young men and maidens, old men and children. For he alone is worthy. His glory is far greater than all of earth and heaven.

TODAY _____

_____

_____

Leviticus 19:32. Luke 2:36, 37. 1 Timothy 5:5. Psalm 148:1, 12, 13.

JUNE

22

Give thanks
to the God
of heaven.

Come before him with thankful
hearts. Let us sing him psalms
of praise. For the Lord is a great
God, the great King of all gods.
He controls the formation of the
depths of the earth and the
mightiest mountains; all are his. He
made the sea and formed the
land; they too are his.

Come, kneel before the Lord
our Maker, for he is our God. We
are his sheep and he is our
Shepherd. Oh, that you would hear
him calling you today and come
to him!

TODAY _____

_____

_____

Psalm 136:26. Psalm 95:2, 3, 4, 5, 6, 7.

How can we describe God?

With what can we compare him?

It is God who sits above the circle of the earth. (The people below must seem to him like grasshoppers!)

Look up into the heavens! Who created all these stars? As a shepherd leads his sheep, calling each by its pet name, and counts them to see that none are lost or strayed, so God does with stars and planets!

How great he is! His power is absolute! His understanding is unlimited.

TODAY _____

_____

_____

Isaiah 40:18a.   Isaiah 40:18b, 22, 26.   Psalm 147:5.

**This is
your wonderful
thought for the day:
Jehovah is God
both in heaven and
down here upon the earth.**

Jehovah is our God, Jehovah
alone. You must love him with
all your heart, soul and might.

I would have you learn this
great fact: that a life of doing right
is the wisest life there is. If you
live that kind of life, you'll not limp
or stumble as you run.

Keep these thoughts ever in
mind; let them penetrate deep
within your heart, for they will
mean real life for you, and
radiant health.

_____ **TODAY**

_____

_____

Deuteronomy 4:39.
Deuteronomy 6:4, 5. Proverbs 4:11, 12, 21.

JUNE

25

Eternal life is in him [Christ].

If being a Christian is of value to us only now in this life, we are the most miserable of creatures. But the fact is that Christ did actually rise from the dead, and has become the first of millions who will come back to life again some day.

So overflowing is his kindness towards us that he took away all our sins through the blood of his Son, by whom we are saved.

God paid a ransom to save you from the impossible road to heaven which your fathers tried to take, and the ransom he paid was not mere gold or silver, as you very well know. But he paid for you with the precious lifeblood of Christ, the sinless, spotless Lamb of God.

TODAY _____

_____

_____

John 1:4.   1 Corinthians 15:19, 20.   Ephesians 1:7.   1 Peter 1:18, 19.

John saw Jesus . . . and said, "Look! There is the Lamb of God who takes away the world's sin!"

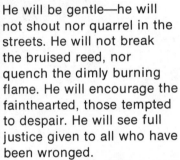

He will be gentle—he will not shout nor quarrel in the streets. He will not break the bruised reed, nor quench the dimly burning flame. He will encourage the fainthearted, those tempted to despair. He will see full justice given to all who have been wronged.

He won't be satisfied until truth and righteousness prevail throughout the earth, nor until even distant lands beyond the seas have put their trust in him.

TODAY _____

_____

_____

John 1:29. Isaiah 42:2, 3, 4.

JUNE

27

Hebrews 2:1.
Hebrews 1:2.
Ephesians 4:15.
Deuteronomy 4:9.

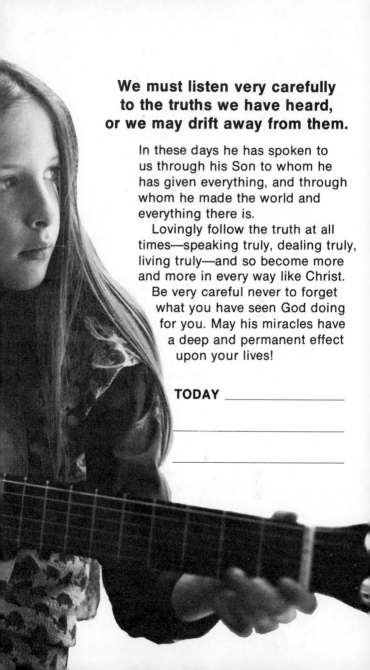

**We must listen very carefully
to the truths we have heard,
or we may drift away from them.**

In these days he has spoken to
us through his Son to whom he
has given everything, and through
whom he made the world and
everything there is.

Lovingly follow the truth at all
times—speaking truly, dealing truly,
living truly—and so become more
and more in every way like Christ.

Be very careful never to forget
what you have seen God doing
for you. May his miracles have
a deep and permanent effect
upon your lives!

TODAY _____

_____

_____

_____

JUNE

28

You must be holy because I, the Lord your God, am holy.

Obey God because you are his children; don't slip back into your old ways—doing evil because you knew no better. But be holy now in everything you do, just as the Lord is holy, who invited you to be his child. He himself has said, "You must be holy, for I am holy."

Throw off your old evil nature. Now your attitudes and thoughts must all be constantly changing for the better. Yes, you must be a new and different person, holy and good.

TODAY _____

_____

_____

Leviticus 19:2. 1 Peter 1:14, 15, 16. Ephesians 4:22, 23, 24.

JUNE

29

The seventh day
is a day of Sabbath rest
before the Lord your God.

If you keep the Sabbath holy,
not having your own fun and
business on that day, but enjoying
the Sabbath and speaking of it
with delight as the Lord's holy day,
and honoring the Lord in what
you do, not following your own
desires and pleasures, nor talking
idly—then the Lord will be your
delight.

Let us not neglect our church
meetings, as some people do,
but encourage and warn each
other, especially now that the
day of his coming back again is
drawing near.

TODAY _____

_____

_____

Exodus 20:10.   Isaiah 58:13, 14.   Hebrews 10:25.

The Lord is coming soon.

Then at last . . . his people will listen to his voice.

Even the hotheads among them will be full of sense and understanding, and those who stammer in uncertainty will speak out plainly.

In those days the ungodly, the atheists, will not be heroes! Wealthy cheaters will not be spoken of as generous, outstanding men! Everyone will recognize an evil man when he sees him, and hypocrites will fool no one at all.

But good men will be generous to others and will be blessed of God for all they do.

TODAY

_____

_____

_____

Philippians 4:5. Isaiah 32:3, 4, 5, 6, 8.

JULY

I am the First and Last; there is no other God.

Who else can tell you what is going to happen in the days ahead? Let them tell you if they can, and prove their power. Let them do as I have done since ancient times.

Is there any other God? No! None that I know about! There is no other Rock!

This is your wonderful thought for the day: Jehovah is God both in heaven and down here upon the earth; and there is no God other than him!

TODAY _____

_____

_____

Isaiah 44:6.   Isaiah 44:7, 8.   Deuteronomy 4:39.

JULY

My words remain forever true.

God's laws are perfect. They
protect us, make us wise, and
give us joy and light.

Think about them every day
and every night so that you will be
sure to obey all of them. For
only then will you succeed. Yes, be
bold and strong. Banish fear and
doubt! For remember, the Lord your
God is with you wherever you go.

I will instruct you (says the
Lord) and guide you along the best
pathway for your life.

_____ **TODAY**

_____

_____

Luke 21:33. Psalm 19:7, 8. Joshua 1:8, 9. Psalm 32:8.

JULY

3

I will bless the Lord and not forget the glorious things he does for me.

He forgives all my sins. He heals me. He ransoms me from hell. He surrounds me with lovingkindness and tender mercies. He fills my life with good things.

What can we ever say to such wonderful things as these? If God is on our side, who can ever be against us? Since he did not spare even his own Son for us but gave him up for us all, won't he also surely give us everything else?

Now glory be to God who by his mighty power at work within us is able to do far more than we would ever dare to ask or even dream of—infinitely beyond our highest prayers, desires, thoughts, or hopes.

TODAY _____

_____

_____

_____

Psalm 103:2.   Psalm 103:3, 4, 5.   Romans 8:31, 32.   Ephesians 3:20.

4

Pray along these lines.

Our Father in heaven, we honor
your holy name.

We ask that your kingdom will
come now. May your will be done
here on earth, just as it is in heaven.

Give us our food again today, as
usual, and forgive us our sins,
just as we have forgiven those who
have sinned against us.

Don't bring us into temptation,
but deliver us from the Evil One.
Amen.

TODAY _____

_____

_____

Matthew 6:9a.   Matthew 6:9b, 10, 11, 12, 13.

**Put on
all of God's armor
so that you will be able
to stand safe
against all strategies
and tricks of Satan.**

For we are not fighting against
people made of flesh and blood,
but against persons without
bodies—the evil rulers of the
unseen world, those mighty satanic
beings and great evil princes of
darkness who rule this world; and
against huge numbers of wicked
spirits in the spirit world.

So use every piece of God's
armor to resist the enemy whenever
he attacks, and when it is all
over, you will still be standing up.

_____ **TODAY**

_____

_____

Ephesians 6:11. Ephesians 6:12, 13.

Run your race to win.

In a race, everyone runs but only one person gets first prize. To win the contest you must deny yourselves many things that would keep you from doing your best.

Run from all these evil things and work instead at what is right and good, learning to trust him and love others, and to be patient and gentle.

Fight well in the Lord's battles . . . Cling tightly to your faith in Christ and always keep your conscience clear, doing what you know is right.

God who began the good work within you will keep right on helping you grow in his grace.

Keep your eyes on Jesus, our leader and instructor.

TODAY

_____

_____

_____

1 Corinthians 9:24b.   1 Corinthians 9:24a, 25.   1 Timothy 6:11.
1 Timothy 1:18, 19.   Philippians 1:6.   Hebrews 12:2.

JULY 7

You have a wonderful future ahead of you.

The good man walks along in the ever-brightening light of God's favor; the dawn gives way to morning splendor.

No mere man has ever seen, heard or even imagined what wonderful things God has ready for those who love the Lord.

Be delighted with the Lord. Then he will give you all your heart's desires. Commit everything you do to the Lord. Trust him to help you do it and he will.

TODAY _____

_____

_____

Proverbs 23:18.   Proverbs 4:18.   1 Corinthians 2:9.   Psalm 37:4, 5.

If you are really eager to give, then it isn't important how much you have to give. God wants you to give what you have, not what you haven't.

It is possible to give away and become richer! It is also possible to hold on too tightly and lose everything.

Take care! Don't do your good deeds publicly, to be admired, for then you will lose the reward from your Father in heaven. When you give a gift to a beggar, don't shout about it . . . do it secretly. And your Father who knows all secrets will reward you.

Cheerful givers are the ones God prizes.

_____ **TODAY**

_____

_____

2 Corinthians 9:7.   2 Corinthians 8:12.   Proverbs 11:24.   Matthew 6:1, 2, 3, 4.

Those who are loving and kind show that they are the children of God.

God loves us, and we feel this warm love everywhere within us because God has given us the Holy Spirit to fill our hearts with his love.

God showed how much he loved us by sending his only Son into this wicked world to bring to us eternal life through his death.

So overflowing is his kindness towards us that he took away all our sins through the blood of his Son, by whom we are saved.

Since God loved us as much as that, we surely ought to love each other.

TODAY _____

_____

1 John 4:7.   Romans 5:5.   1 John 4:9.   Ephesians 1:7.   1 John 4:11.

Give to those who ask, and don't turn away from those who want to borrow.

There is a saying, "Love your *friends* and hate your enemies." But I say: Love your *enemies*! Pray for those who *persecute* you! In that way you will be acting as true sons of your Father in heaven. For he gives his sunlight to both the evil and the good, and sends rain on the just and on the unjust too.

If you love only those who love you, what good is that? Even scoundrels do that much.

If you are friendly only to your friends, how are you different from anyone else?

TODAY _____

_____

_____

Matthew 5:42. Matthew 5:43, 44, 45, 46, 47.

JULY

11

One's nationality or race or education or social position is unimportant.

Such things mean nothing.
Whether a person has Christ is
what matters, and he is equally
available to all.

Since you have been chosen by
God . . . and because of his
deep love and concern for you, you
should practice tenderhearted
mercy and kindness to others.

May the Lord make your love
to grow and overflow to each other
. . . This will result in your
hearts being made strong, sinless
and holy by God our Father, so
that you may stand before him
guiltless on that day when our
Lord Jesus Christ returns.

TODAY _____

_____

_____

Colossians 3:11a.   Colossians 3:11b, 12.   1 Thessalonians 3:12, 13.

The Lord is coming soon.

With this news bring cheer to all discouraged ones. Encourage those who are afraid. Tell them, "Be strong, fear not, for your God is coming to destroy your enemies. He is coming to save you."

And when he comes, he will open the eyes of the blind, and unstop the ears of the deaf. The lame man will leap up like a deer, and those who could not speak will shout and sing!

Springs will burst forth in the wilderness, and streams in the desert.

TODAY _____

_____

_____

Philippians 4:5.   Isaiah 35:3, 4, 5, 6.

**The Lord
of Hosts
is a wonderful
teacher
and gives
the farmer
wisdom.**

Does a farmer
always plow and
never sow? Is he
forever harrowing the soil and never
planting it? Does he not finally
plant his many kinds of grain, each
in its own section of his land?
He knows just what to do, for God
has made him see and understand.
O Lord, what miracles you do!
And how deep are your thoughts!
You have all wisdom and do
great and mighty miracles; for your
eyes are open to all the ways of
men, and you reward everyone
according to his life and deeds.

TODAY _____

_____

Isaiah 28:29.   Isaiah 28:23, 24, 25, 26.   Psalm 92:5.   Jeremiah 32:19.

JULY

**"I will cut off
the strength
of evil men,"
says the Lord.**

What a slippery path they
are on—suddenly God will send
them sliding over the edge of the
cliff and down to their destruction:
an instant end to all their
happiness, an eternity of terror.
Their present life is only a dream!

But the good man walks along
in the ever-brightening light of
God's favor; the dawn gives way
to morning splendor.

_____ **TODAY**

_____

_____

Psalm 75:10.   Psalm 73:18, 19, 20.   Proverbs 4:18.

We can be mirrors that brightly reflect the glory of the Lord.

And as the Spirit of the Lord works within us, we become more and more like him.

We are able to hold our heads high no matter what happens and know that all is well, for we know how dearly God loves us, and we feel this warm love everywhere within us because God has given us the Holy Spirit to fill our hearts with his love.

If we are living now by the Holy Spirit's power, let us follow the Holy Spirit's leading in every part of our lives.

_____ **TODAY**

_____

_____

2 Corinthians 3:18.   Romans 5:5.   Galatians 5:25.

JULY

**Leave behind
your foolishness
and begin to live;
learn how to be wise.**

Remember your leaders who
have taught you the Word of
God. Think of all the good that has
come from their lives, and try to
trust the Lord as they do.

Obey your spiritual leaders and
be willing to do what they say. For
their work is to watch over your
souls, and God will judge them on
how well they do this. Give them
reason to report joyfully about you
to the Lord.

The value of wisdom is far above
rubies; nothing can be compared
with it.

TODAY _____

_____

_____

Proverbs 9:6.   Hebrews 13:7, 17.   Proverbs 8:11.

JULY

17

**All who
listen to
my instructions
and follow them
are wise.**

God's laws are perfect. They
protect us, make us wise, and
give us joy and light. God's laws
are pure, eternal, just. They are
more desirable than gold. They are
sweeter than honey dripping
from a honeycomb. For they warn
us away from harm and give
success to those who obey them.

For all God's words are right,
and everything he does is worthy
of our trust. He loves whatever is
just and good; the earth is filled
with his tender love.

_____ **TODAY**

_____

_____

Matthew 7:24.   Psalm 19:7, 8, 9, 10, 11.   Psalm 33:4, 5.

Despise God's Word and find yourself in trouble. Obey it and succeed.

Obeying these commandments is not something beyond your strength and reach.

Remember this—the wrong desires that come into your life aren't anything new and different. Many others have faced exactly the same problems before you. And no temptation is irresistible. You can trust God to keep the temptation from becoming so strong that you can't stand up against it, for he has promised this and will do what he says.

Choose to love the Lord your God and to obey him and to cling to him, for he is your life and the length of your days.

_____ **TODAY**

_____

_____

Proverbs 13:13. Deuteronomy 30:11. 1 Corinthians 10:13. Deuteronomy 30:20.

JULY

19

**If any of you
wants to be my follower,
you must put aside
your own pleasures
and shoulder your cross,
and follow me closely.**

If you insist on saving your life,
you will lose it. Only those who
throw away their lives for my sake
and for the sake of the Good
News will ever know what it means
to really live.

And how does a man benefit if
he gains the whole world and
loses his soul in the process? For
is anything worth more than his
soul?

And anyone who is ashamed of
me and my message in these days
of unbelief and sin, I, the Messiah,
will be ashamed of him when
I return in the glory of my
Father, with the holy angels.

_____ **TODAY**

_____

_____

Mark 8:34.   Mark 8:35, 36, 37, 38.

Don't fail
to do these things
that God entrusted
to you.

King Hezekiah handled the
distribution throughout all Judah,
doing what was just and fair in the
sight of the Lord his God. He
worked very hard to encourage
respect for the Temple, the law,
and godly living, and was very
successful.

Keep me far from every wrong;
help me, undeserving as I am, to
obey your laws, for I have chosen
to do right. I cling to your
commands and follow them as closely
as I can. Lord, don't let me
make a mess of things.

TODAY _____

_____

_____

1 Timothy 6:20. 2 Chronicles 31:20, 21. Psalm 119:29, 30, 31.

JULY 27

Remind me of this promise of forgiveness, for we must talk about your sins. Plead your case for my forgiving you.

Come, let's talk this over! says the Lord; no matter how deep the stain of your sins, I can take it out and make you as clean as freshly fallen snow.

I, yes, I alone am he who blots away your sins for my own sake and will never think of them again.

The blood of Christ will transform our lives and hearts . . . For by the help of the eternal Holy Spirit, Christ willingly gave himself to God to die for our sins—he being perfect, without a single sin or fault.

TODAY _____

_____

Isaiah 43:25.   Isaiah 43:26.   Isaiah 1:18.   Hebrews 9:14.

**Salvation that comes
from trusting Christ . . .
is already within
easy reach of us;
in fact, it is as near
as our own hearts and mouths.**

For if you tell others with your
own mouth that Jesus Christ is
your Lord, and believe in your own
heart that God has raised him
from the dead, you will be saved.

For it is by believing in his
heart that a man becomes right
with God; and with his mouth
he tells others of his faith, confirming
his salvation.

For the Scriptures tell us that no
one who believes in Christ will
ever be disappointed.

Anyone who calls upon the
name of the Lord will be saved.

TODAY _____

_____

_____

Romans 10:8.   Romans 10:9, 10, 11, 13.

JULY

23

**I will tell you new things
I haven't mentioned before,
secrets you haven't heard.**

For I know the plans I have for
you, says the Lord. They are
plans for good and not for evil, to
give you a future and a hope.

This plan of mine is not what
you would work out, neither are
my thoughts the same as yours!
For just as the heavens are
higher than the earth, so are my
ways higher than yours, and my
thoughts than yours.

Come to me with your ears
wide open.

TODAY _____

_____

_____

Isaiah 48:6. Jeremiah 29:11. Isaiah 55:8, 9, 3.

Anne Thielking, age 11

JULY

24

My sheep recognize my voice.

When Jesus came by he looked up at Zacchaeus and called him by name! "Zacchaeus," he said, "Quick! Come down! For I am going to be a guest in your house today!" Zacchaeus hurriedly climbed down and took Jesus to his house in great excitement and joy.

I have been standing at the door and I am constantly knocking. If anyone hears me calling him and opens the door, I will come in and fellowship with him and he with me.

Then at last they will recognize that it is I, yes, I, who speaks to them.

_____ **TODAY**

_____

_____

John 10:27. Luke 19:5, 6. Revelation 3:20. Isaiah 52:6.

JULY

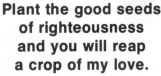

Plant the good seeds of righteousness and you will reap a crop of my love.

Love your *enemies*! Do good to *them*! Lend to *them*! And don't be concerned about the fact that they won't repay. Then your reward from heaven will be very great, and you will truly be acting as sons of God.

Try to show as much compassion as your Father does.

For if you give, you will get! Your gift will return to you in full and overflowing measure, pressed down, shaken together to make room for more, and running over. Whatever measure you use to give—large or small—will be used to measure what is given back to you.

TODAY _____

_____

_____

Hosea 10:12. Luke 6:35, 36, 38.

JULY

**Don't always be trying
to get out of
doing your duty,
even when
it's unpleasant.**

Obey your parents; this is the
right thing to do because God
has placed them in authority
over you.

Obey your spiritual leaders and
be willing to do what they say.

Obey the government and its
officers, and always . . . be
obedient and ready for any honest
work.

Show respect for everyone. Love
Christians everywhere. Fear God
and honor the government.

Pray . . . for kings and all
others who are in authority.

TODAY _____

_____

_____

Ecclesiastes 8:2. Ephesians 6:1. Hebrews 12:17. Titus 3:1. 1 Peter 2:17. 1 Timothy 2:2.

JULY

27

The policeman is sent by God to help you.

Obey the government, for God is the one who has put it there. There is no government anywhere that God has not placed in power. So those who refuse to obey the laws of the land are refusing to obey God, and punishment will follow.

For the policeman does not frighten people who are doing right; but those doing evil will always fear him. So if you don't want to be afraid, keep the laws and you will get along well.

Obey the laws, then, for two reasons: first, to keep from being punished, and second, just because you know you should.

TODAY _____

_____

_____

Romans 13:4. Romans 13:1, 2, 3, 5.

JULY 28

A blow to the nose causes bleeding, so anger causes quarrels.

Stop being mean, bad-tempered and angry. Quarreling, harsh words, and dislike of others should have no place in your lives.

Instead, be kind to each other, tenderhearted, forgiving one another, just as God has forgiven you because you belong to Christ.

Be full of love for others, following the example of Christ who loved you and gave himself to God as a sacrifice to take away your sins.

And so I am giving a new commandment to you now—love each other just as much as I love you. Your strong love for each other will prove to the world that you are my disciples.

TODAY _____

_____

_____

Proverbs 30:33. Ephesians 4:31, 32. Ephesians 5:2. John 13:34, 35.

**Never forget the things
I've taught you.
If you want
a long and satisfying life,
closely follow my instructions.**

You must keep on believing the
things you have been taught.
You know how, when you were a
small child, you were taught the
holy Scriptures; and it is these that
make you wise to accept God's
salvation by trusting in Christ
Jesus.

The whole Bible was given to us
by inspiration from God and is
useful to teach us what is true and
to make us realize what is wrong
in our lives; it straightens us out
and helps us do what is right.

It is God's way of making us well
prepared at every point, fully
equipped to do good to everyone.

TODAY _____

_____

_____

Proverbs 3:1, 2.   2 Timothy 3:14, 15, 16, 17.

JULY

**Search
the Book
of the Lord.**

Keep these commandments
carefully in mind. Tie them to
your hand to remind you to obey
them, and tie them to your
forehead between your eyes!

Think about them every day
and every night so that you will be
sure to obey all of them. For
only then will you succeed.

I have thought much about
your words, and stored them in my
heart so that they would hold me
back from sin.

_____ **TODAY**

_____

_____

Isaiah 34:16. Deuteronomy 11:18. Joshua 1:8. Psalm 119:11.

© 1957 United Feature Syndicate, Inc.

Never criticize
or condemn—
or it will all
come back on you.

Go easy on others; then they will
do the same for you.

For others will treat you as you
treat them.

And why worry about a speck in
the eye of a brother when you
have a board in your own? Should
you say, 'Friend, let me help you
get that speck out of your eye,'
when you can't even see
because of the board in your own?
Hypocrite! First get rid of the
board. Then you can see to help
your brother.

TODAY _____

_____

_____

Luke 6:37. Matthew 7:2, 3, 4, 5.

See the way
God does things and fall into line.
Don't fight the facts of nature.

Quit quarreling with God! Agree
with him and you will have peace at
last! His favor will surround you if
you will only admit that you were
wrong.

Do the good things that result
from being saved, obeying God
with deep reverence, shrinking
back from all that might displease
him. For God is at work within
you, helping you want to obey him,
and then helping you do what he
wants.

"I know the plans I have for
you," says the Lord. "They are
plans for good and not for evil."

TODAY _____

_____

_____

Ecclesiastes 7:13.   Job 22:21.   Philippians 2:12, 13.   Jeremiah 29:11.

AUGUST

Try to
find out and do
whatever the Lord
wants you to.

God wants you to be holy and pure.
It was a happy day for him when
he gave us our new lives,
through the truth of his Word. So
get rid of all that is wrong in
your life, both inside and outside.

[Jesus] said, " . . . Anyone
who does God's will is my brother,
and my sister, and my mother."

All who listen to my instructions
and follow them are wise, like a
man who builds his house on solid
rock. Though the rain comes in
torrents, and the floods rise and
the storm winds beat against his
house, it won't collapse, for it is
built on rock.

TODAY _____

_____

_____

Ephesians 5:17.
1 Thessalonians 4:3.   James 1:18, 21.   Mark 3:34, 35.   Matthew 7:24, 25.

Your sins have cut you off from God.

Your ways have brought this
down upon you; it is a bitter
dose of your own medicine, striking
deep within your hearts.

No one has ever really followed
God's paths, or even truly
wanted to. Every one has turned
away; all have gone wrong.

O Lord, I know it is not within
the power of man to map his life
and plan his course—so you
correct me, Lord; but please be
gentle.

TODAY _____

_____

_____

Isaiah 59:2.   Jeremiah 4:18.   Romans 3:11, 12.   Jeremiah 10:23, 24.

AUGUST

4

I will not . . . fail

God is not a man, that he should lie; he doesn't change his mind like humans do. Has he ever promised without doing what he said?

The Lord your God is the faithful God who for a thousand generations keeps his promises and constantly loves those who love him and who obey his commands.

He never forgets his promises.

So don't be anxious about tomorrow. God will take care of your tomorrow too. Live one day at a time.

He is a mighty Savior . . . he will love you and not accuse you.

Go to God and confess your sins to him. For he does wonderful miracles, marvels without number.

TODAY _____

_____

_____

Joshua 1:5.   Numbers 23:19.   Deuteronomy 7:9.   Psalm 111:5.   Matthew 6:34.
Zephaniah 3:17, 18.   Job 5:8, 9.

to help you.

AUGUST

5

Who . . . holds the wind in his fists?

Who else but God? . . . Who but God has created the world?

For you are dealing with the one who formed the mountains and made the winds, and knows your every thought; he turns the morning to darkness and crushes down the mountains underneath his feet: Jehovah, the Lord, the God of Hosts, is his name.

He is high above the nations; his glory is far greater than the heavens. Who can be compared with God enthroned on high?

_____ **TODAY**

_____

_____

Proverbs 30:4. Amos 4:13. Psalm 113:4, 5.

Many people can build houses, but only God made everything.

The heavens are telling the glory of God; they are a marvelous display of his craftsmanship.

He merely spoke, and the heavens were formed, and all the galaxies of stars. He made the oceans, pouring them into his vast reservoirs. When he but spoke, the world began! It appeared at his command!

All the peoples of the world are nothing in comparison with him—they are but a drop in the bucket, dust on the scales. He picks up the islands as though they had no weight at all.

Who else has held the oceans in his hands and measured off the heavens with his ruler? Who else knows the weight of all the earth and weighs the mountains and the hills?

TODAY _____

_____

_____

Hebrews 3:4. Psalm 19:1. Psalm 33:6, 7, 9. Isaiah 40:15, 12.

AUGUST
7

God is Light and in him is no darkness at all.

So if we say we are his friends, but go on living in spiritual darkness and sin, we are lying.

And how can we be sure that we belong to him? By looking within ourselves: are we really trying to do what he wants us to?

Someone may say, "I am a Christian; I am on my way to heaven; I belong to Christ." But if he doesn't do what Christ tells him to, he is a liar. But those who do what Christ tells them to will learn to love God more and more. That is the way to know whether or not you are a Christian. Anyone who says he is a Christian should live as Christ did.

TODAY _____

_____

_____

1 John 1:5, 6.   1 John 2:3, 4, 5, 6.

**Live a life of steady goodness,
so that only good deeds will pour forth.
And if you don't brag about them,
then you will be truly wise!**

Happy are all who perfectly
follow the laws of God. Happy
are all who search for God, and
always do his will, rejecting
compromise with evil, and walking
only in his paths.

The more lowly your service to
others, the greater you are. To
be the greatest, be a servant. But
those who think themselves great
shall be disappointed and humbled;
and those who humble
themselves shall be exalted.

TODAY _____

_____

_____

James 3:13. Psalm 119:1, 2, 3. Matthew 23:11, 12.

**Do things
in such a way
that everyone
can see you
are honest
clear through.**

For though once your heart was full of darkness, now it is full of light from the Lord, and your behavior should show it! Because of this light within you, you should do only what is good and right and true.   Do for others what you want them to do for you.

   All who are honest and fair . . . such as these shall dwell on high.

TODAY _____

_____

_____

Romans 12:17. Ephesians 5:8, 9. Matthew 7:12. Isaiah 33:15, 16.

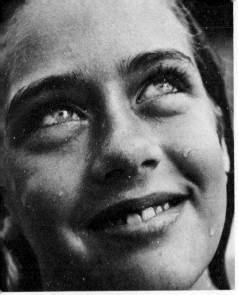

The Lord is coming soon.

In that day the deaf will hear the words of a book, and out of their gloom and darkness the blind will see my plans. The meek will be filled with fresh joy from the Lord, and the poor shall exult in the Holy One of Israel. Bullies will vanish and scoffers will cease.

Those in error will believe the truth and complainers will be willing to be taught!

_____ **TODAY**

_____

_____

Philippians 4:5. Isaiah 29:18, 19, 20, 24.

AUGUST

11

**Never abandon
a friend—
either yours
or your father's.**

Give what you have to anyone
who asks you for it; and when
things are taken away from you,
don't worry about getting them
back. Treat others as you want
them to treat you.

Do you think you deserve credit
for merely loving those who love
you? Even the godless do that!

Share each other's troubles
and problems, and so obey our
Lord's command. If anyone
thinks he is too great to stoop to
this, he is fooling himself. He is
really a nobody.

_____ **TODAY**

_____

_____

Proverbs 27:10. Luke 6:30, 31, 32. Galatians 6:2, 3.

AUGUST

12

If God
has given you money,
be generous
in helping others
with it.

For if you give, you will get!
Your gift will return to you in
full and overflowing measure,
pressed down, shaken together
to make room for more, and
running over. Whatever measure
you use to give—large or
small—will be used to measure
what is given back to you.

Remember this—if you give
little, you will get little. A farmer
who plants just a few seeds will
get only a small crop, but if he
plants much, he will reap much.

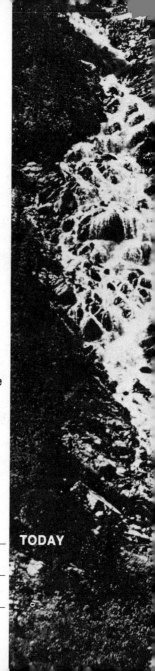

TODAY

Romans 12:8. Luke 6:38. 2 Corinthians 9:6.

AUGUST

Roll a boulder down on someone, and it will roll back and crush you.

For others will treat you as you treat them.

There will be no mercy to those who have shown no mercy.

Never criticize or condemn—or it will all come back on you. Go easy on others; then they will do the same for you.

Keep a close watch on all you do and think. Stay true to what is right and God will bless you and use you to help others.

So see to it that you really do love each other warmly, with all your hearts.

TODAY

_____

_____

_____

Proverbs 26:27. Matthew 7:2. James 2:13.
Luke 6:37. 1 Peter 1:22. 1 Timothy 4:16.

Gossip separates the best of friends.

The tongue is a small thing, but what enormous damage it can do. A great forest can be set on fire by one tiny spark. And the tongue is a flame of fire. The tongue . . . can turn our whole lives into a blazing flame of destruction and disaster. It is always ready to pour out its deadly poison.

Now is the time to cast off and throw away all these rotten garments of anger, hatred, cursing, and dirty language. Don't tell lies to each other.

Some people like to make cutting remarks, but the words of the wise soothe and heal. Truth stands the test of time; lies are soon exposed.

_____ **TODAY**

_____

_____

Proverbs 16:28. James 3:5, 6, 8. Colossians 3:8, 9. Proverbs 12:18, 19.

Happy are those who strive for peace— they shall be called the sons of God.

"The law of Moses says, 'If a man gouges out another's eye, he must pay with his own eye. If a tooth gets knocked out, knock out the tooth of the one who did it.' But I [Jesus] say: Don't resist violence! If you are slapped on one cheek, turn the other too."

A soft answer turns away wrath, but harsh words cause quarrels. It is better to be slow-tempered than famous; it is better to have self-control than to control an army.

TODAY _____

_____

_____

Matthew 5:9. Matthew 5:38, 39. Proverbs 15:1. Proverbs 16:32.

**Why quibble
about the speck
in someone else's eye—
his little fault—
when a board
is in your own?**

Show as much compassion as
your Father does. Never criticize
or condemn—or it will all come
back on you. Go easy on others;
then they will do the same for you.

Practice tenderhearted mercy
and kindness to others. . . . Be
gentle and ready to forgive;
never hold grudges.

Let love guide your life.

TODAY _____

_____

_____

Luke 6:41. Luke 6:36, 37. Colossians 3:12, 13, 14.

Work happily together. Don't try to act big.

Don't try to get into the good graces of important people, but enjoy the company of ordinary folks. And don't think you know it all!

Never pay back evil for evil. Do things in such a way that everyone can see you are honest clear through.

Don't quarrel with anyone. Be at peace with everyone, just as much as possible.

Don't just pretend that you love others: really love them. Hate what is wrong. Stand on the side of the good. Love each other with brotherly affection and take delight in honoring each other.

You have no right to criticize your brother or look down on him. Remember, each of us will stand personally before the Judgment Seat of God.

_____ **TODAY**

_____

_____

For I really want to do what is right, but I can't. I do what I don't want to—what I hate. I know perfectly well that what I am doing is wrong, and my bad conscience proves that I agree with these laws I am breaking.

No matter which way I turn I can't make myself do right. I want to but I can't.

It seems to be a fact of life that when I want to do what is right, I inevitably do what is wrong.

God is at work within you, helping you want to obey him, and then helping you do what he wants.

I don't understand myself at all.

_____ **TODAY**

_____

_____

Romans 7:15a.   Romans 7:15b, 16, 18, 21.   Philippians 2:13.

You have a new life.

It was not passed on to you from your parents, for the life they gave you will fade away. This new one will last forever, for it comes from Christ, God's ever-living Message to men. Yes, our natural lives will fade as grass does when it becomes all brown and dry. All our greatness is like a flower that droops and falls; but the Word of the Lord will last forever.

Come to Christ, who is the living Foundation of Rock upon which God builds; though men have spurned him, he is very precious to God who has chosen him above all others.

TODAY _____

_____

_____

1 Peter 1:23a.   1 Peter 1:23b, 24, 25.   1 Peter 2:4.

AUGUST

20

**If you are unwilling
to obey the Lord,
then decide today
whom you will obey.**

When Rehoboam was at the height of his popularity and power he abandoned the Lord, and the people followed him in this sin.

He was an evil king, for he never did decide really to please the Lord.

I am giving you the choice today between God's blessing or God's curse! There will be blessing if you obey the commandments of the Lord your God . . . and a curse if you refuse them.

Oh, that you would choose life . . . Choose to love the Lord your God.

TODAY _____

_____

_____

Joshua 24:15.
2 Chronicles 12:1, 14.   Deuteronomy 11:26, 27, 28.   Deuteronomy 30:19, 20.

**Live within
God's circle
of blessing.**

Stay always within the
boundaries where God's love can
reach and bless you. Wait patiently
for the eternal life that our Lord
Jesus Christ in his mercy is going
to give you.

Try to help those who argue
against you. Be merciful to those
who doubt . . . Help them to find
the Lord by being kind to them,
but be careful that you yourselves
aren't pulled along into their sins.

[God] is able to keep you from
slipping and falling away, and to
bring you, sinless and perfect,
into his glorious presence.

TODAY _____

_____

_____

Psalm 25:13. Jude 21, 22, 23, 25.

AUGUST

**Do not
defile yourselves
by consulting
mediums
and wizards,
for I am Jehovah
your God.**

I will set my face against anyone who consults mediums and wizards instead of me.

Can the living find out the future from the dead? Why not ask your God?

If we are living now by the Holy Spirit's power, let us follow the Holy Spirit's leading in every part of our lives.

Stand firm and keep a strong grip on the truth.

TODAY _____

_____

_____

Leviticus 19:31.   Leviticus 20:6.   Isaiah 8:19.   Galatians 5:25.   2 Thessalonians 2:15.

**Live no longer
as the unsaved do,
for they are blinded
and confused.**

Their closed hearts are full of
darkness; they are far away from
the life of God because they have
shut their minds against him,
and they cannot understand his
ways.

But that isn't the way Christ
taught you! Your attitudes and
thoughts must all be constantly
changing for the better. Yes, you
must be a new and different
person, holy and good. Clothe
yourself with this new nature.

_____ **TODAY**

_____

_____

Ephesians 4:17a.   Ephesians 4:17b, 18, 20, 23, 24.

TODAY

Listen to my counsel— oh, don't refuse it— and be wise.

"All who listen to my instructions and follow them are wise, like a man who builds his house on solid rock. Though the rain comes in torrents, and the floods rise and the storm winds beat against his house, it won't collapse, for it is built on rock.

"But those who hear my instructions and ignore them are foolish, like a man who builds his house on sand. For when the rains and floods come, and storm winds beat against his house, it will fall with a mighty crash."

The crowds were amazed at Jesus' sermons, for he taught as one who had great authority.

_____

_____

_____

Proverbs 8:33.   Matthew 7:24, 25, 26, 27, 28, 29.

AUGUST

25

There has never been another prophet like Moses.

It was by faith that Moses, when he grew up, refused to be treated as the grandson of the king, but chose to share ill-treatment with God's people instead of enjoying the fleeting pleasures of sin. He thought that it was better to suffer for the promised Christ than to own all the treasures of Egypt, for he was looking forward to the great reward that God would give him.

And it was because he trusted God that he left the land of Egypt and wasn't afraid of the king's anger. Moses kept right on going; it seemed as though he could see God right there with him.

TODAY _____

_____

Deuteronomy 34:10.   Hebrews 11:24, 25, 26, 27.

These men of faith . . . won [God's] approval.

. . . Gideon and Barak and Samson and Jephthah and David and Samuel and all the other prophets.

These people all trusted God and as a result won battles, overthrew kingdoms, ruled their people well, and received what God had promised them.

Some, through their faith, escaped death by the sword. Some were made strong again after they had been weak or sick. Others were given great power in battle; they made whole armies turn and run away.

TODAY _____

_____

Hebrews 11:39.   Hebrews 11:32, 33, 34.

The Lord
is my light
and my salvation;
whom shall I fear?

Jehovah is my rock, my fortress
and my Savior. I will hide in
God, who is my rock and my
refuge. He is my shield and my
salvation, my refuge and high
tower.

He is my strength, my shield
from every danger. I trusted in
him, and he helped me.

That is why we can say
without any doubt or fear, "The
Lord is my Helper and I am not
afraid of anything that mere man
can do to me."

TODAY _____

_____

_____

Psalm 27:1.   2 Samuel 22:2, 3.   Psalm 28:7.   Hebrews 13:6.

Fear of man is a dangerous trap, but to trust in God means safety.

Two of the spies, Joshua . . . and Caleb . . . said to all the people, "It is a wonderful country ahead, and the Lord loves us. He will bring us safely into the land and give it to us. Do not fear the people of the land."

But the only response of the people was to talk of stoning them.

Usually no one will hurt you for wanting to do good. But even if they should you are to be envied, for God will reward you for it. Quietly trust yourself to Christ your Lord.

TODAY _____

_____

_____

Proverbs 29:25.   Numbers 14:6, 7, 8, 9, 10.   1 Peter 3:13, 14, 15.

AUGUST 29

Pray along these lines:
"Our Father in heaven."

Jesus . . . looked up to heaven and said, "Father."

We are all children of God through faith in Jesus Christ.

And because we are his sons God has sent the Spirit of his Son into our hearts, so now we can rightly speak of God as our dear Father.

And so we should not be like cringing, fearful slaves, but we should behave like God's very own children.

I [God] will welcome you, and be a Father to you, and you will be my sons and daughters.

TODAY _____

_____

_____

Matthew 6:9.   John 17:1.   Galatians 3:26.   Galatians 4:6.   Romans 8:15.
2 Corinthians 6:17, 18.

**There are
different kinds
of service to God.**

Our bodies have many parts, but
the many parts make up only
one body when they are all put
together. So it is with the
"body" of Christ. Each of us is a
part of the one body of Christ.

Don't let anyone think little of
you because you are young. Be
their ideal; let them follow the way
you teach and live; be a pattern
for them in your love, your faith,
and your clean thoughts.

It is the same Lord we are serving.

TODAY _____

_____

1 Corinthians 12:5.   1 Corinthians 12:12, 13.   1 Timothy 4:12.   1 Corinthians 12:5.

AUGUST
31

Don't be proud
of following the wise men
of this world.

For God in his wisdom saw to it
that the world would never find
God through human brilliance.

It seems foolish to the Jews
because they want a sign from
heaven as proof that what is
preached is true; and it is foolish
to the Gentiles because they
believe only what agrees with their
philosophy and seems wise to
them.

In the book of Psalms, we are
told that the Lord knows full well
how the human mind reasons,
and how foolish and futile it is.

For it is from God alone that
you have your life through Christ
Jesus. He showed us God's plan
of salvation; he was the one who
made us acceptable to God.

TODAY _____

_____

_____

1 Corinthians 3:21.   1 Corinthians 1:21, 22.   1 Corinthians 3:20.   1 Corinthians 1:30.

Honor
your father and mother,
that you may have
a long, good life.

Obey your parents; this is the
right thing to do because God
has placed them in authority over
you. Honor your father and
mother. This is the first of God's
Ten Commandments that ends
with a promise. And this is the
promise: that if you
honor your father and
mother, yours will be a
long life,
full of
blessing.

Make your bed.

Joy Harrison, age 10

Tie their
instructions around your
finger so you won't forget. Take
to heart all of their advice. What
you learn from them will stand
you in good stead; it will gain you
many honors.

TODAY

Exodus 20:12. Ephesians 6:1, 2, 3. Proverbs 6:21. Proverbs 1:9.

SEPTEMBER

The good man walks along in the ever-brightening light of God's favor.

Oh, the joys of those who do not follow evil men's advice, who do not hang around with sinners, scoffing at the things of God:

But they delight in doing everything God wants them to, and day and night are always meditating on his laws and thinking about ways to follow him more closely.

They are like trees along a river bank bearing luscious fruit each season without fail. Their leaves shall never wither, and all they do shall prosper.

TODAY _____

_____

Proverbs 4:18. Psalm 1:1, 2, 3.

**The Lord says:
Cursed is the man
who puts his trust
in mortal man
and turns his heart
away from God.**

He is like a stunted shrub in the
desert, with no hope for the
future; he lives on the
salt-encrusted plains in the
barren wilderness; good times pass
him by forever.

But blessed is the man who
trusts in the Lord and has made
the Lord his hope and confidence.
He is like a tree planted along a
riverbank, with its roots reaching
deep into the water—a tree not
bothered by the heat nor worried
by long months of drought. Its
leaves stay green and it goes right
on producing all its luscious fruit.

TODAY _____

_____

_____

Jeremiah 17:5.   Jeremiah 17:6, 7, 8.

**When I am afraid,
I will put
my confidence
in you.**

Peter went over the side of the boat and walked on the water toward Jesus. But when he looked around at the high waves, he was terrified and began to sink. "Save me, Lord!" he shouted. Instantly Jesus reached out his hand and rescued him.

O Jehovah, Commander of the heavenly armies, where is there any other Mighty One like you? You rule the oceans when their waves arise in fearful storms; you speak and they lie still.

You are mightier than all the breakers pounding on the seashores of the world!

TODAY

_____

_____

_____

Psalm 56:3. Matthew 14:29, 30, 31. Psalm 89:8, 9. Psalm 93:4.

Who . . . can ever keep Christ's love from us?

When we have trouble or calamity, when we are hunted down or destroyed, is it because he doesn't love us anymore? And if we are hungry, or penniless, or in danger, or threatened with death, has God deserted us?

I am convinced that nothing can ever separate us from his love. Death can't, and life can't. The angels won't, and all the powers of hell itself cannot keep God's love away. Our fears for today, our worries about tomorrow, or where we are—high above the sky, or in the deepest ocean—nothing will ever be able to separate us from the love of God demonstrated by our Lord Jesus Christ when he died for us.

TODAY _____

_____

_____

Romans 8:35a.   Romans 8:35b, 38, 39.

No one can follow me in and slay me. He is a rugged mountain where I hide; he is my Savior, a rock where none can reach me, and a tower of safety. He is my shield.

What a God he is! How perfect in every way! All his promises prove true. He is a shield for everyone who hides behind him. For who is God except our Lord? Who but he is as a rock?

The Lord is my fort where I can enter and be safe.

_____ **TODAY**

_____

_____

Psalm 18:2a. Psalm 18:2b, 30.

Because
the Lord is my Shepherd,
I have everything I need!

He lets me rest in the meadow
grass and leads me beside the
quiet streams. He restores my
failing health. He helps me do
what honors him the most.

Even when walking through the
dark valley of death I will not be
afraid, for you are close beside
me, guarding, guiding all the way.

You provide delicious food for
me in the presence of my enemies.
You have welcomed me as your
guest; blessings overflow!

Your goodness and unfailing
kindness shall be with me all of my
life, and afterwards I will live
with you forever in your home.

TODAY _____

_____

_____

Psalm 23:1.   Psalm 23:2, 3, 4, 5, 6.

SEPTEMBER

The heavens are telling the glory of God; they are a marvelous display of his craftsmanship.

Since earliest times men have seen the earth and sky and all God made, and have known of his existence and great eternal power.

When I look up into the night skies and see the work of your fingers—the moon and the stars you have made—I cannot understand how you can bother with mere puny man, to pay any attention to him!

Day and night they keep on telling about God. Without a sound or word, silent in the skies, their message reaches out to all the world.

And those who are wise—the people of God—shall shine as brightly as the sun's brilliance, and those who turn many to righteousness will glitter like stars forever.

TODAY _____

_____

_____

Psalm 19:1.   Romans 1:20.   Psalm 8:3, 4.   Psalm 19:2, 3, 4.   Daniel 12:3.

SEPTEMBER

9

The earth belongs to God.

Everything in all the world is his!
He is the one who pushed the
oceans back to let dry land appear.
  Who may climb the mountain
of the Lord and enter where he
lives? Who may stand before the
Lord? Only those with pure hands
and hearts, who do not practice
dishonesty and lying. They will
receive God's own goodness as
their blessing from him, planted in
their lives by God himself, their
Savior. These are the ones who are
allowed to stand before the Lord
and worship the God of Jacob.

TODAY _____

_____

Psalm 24:1a. Psalm 24:1b, 2, 3, 4, 5, 6.

Believe in Christ
and fully trust him.

The Lord sent poisonous snakes
among [the people of Israel] to
punish them, and many of them
were bitten and died. Then the
people came to Moses and cried
out, "We have sinned."

Then the Lord told him, "Make a
bronze replica of one of these
snakes and attach it to the top of
a pole; anyone who is bitten
shall live if he simply looks at it!"

And as Moses in the
wilderness lifted up the bronze
image of a serpent on a pole,
even so I [Jesus] must be lifted up
upon a pole, so that anyone who
believes in me will have eternal life.

TODAY _____

_____

_____

Galatians 3:5. Numbers 21:6, 7, 8. John 3:14, 15.

SEPTEMBER

**No one is good—
no one in all the world
is innocent.**

Every one has turned away; all
have gone wrong. No one
anywhere has kept on doing what
is right; not one.

All have sinned; all fall short of
God's glorious ideal; yet now
God declares us "not guilty" of
offending him if we trust in
Jesus Christ, who in his kindness
freely takes away our sins.

Who then will condemn us?

TODAY _____

_____

_____

Romans 3:10. Romans 3:12, 23, 24. Romans 8:34.

**Long ago,
even before
he made the world,
God chose us
to be his very own,
through what Christ
would do for us.**

He decided then to make us holy
in his eyes, without a single
fault—we who stand before him
covered with his love. His
unchanging plan has always been
to adopt us into his own family
by sending Jesus Christ to die for
us. And he did this because he
wanted to!

So overflowing is his kindness
towards us that he took away all
our sins through the blood of his
Son, by whom we are saved; and
he has showered down upon us
the richness of his grace—for how
well he understands us and
knows what is best for us at all
times.

TODAY _____

_____

_____

Ephesians 1:4a.   Ephesians 1:4b, 5, 7, 8.

SEPTEMBER 13

**God has given us
the Holy Spirit
to fill our hearts
with his love.**

Our love for him comes as a
result of his loving us first.

God is love, and anyone who
lives in love is living with God
and God is living in him.

Continue to show deep love
for each other, for love makes up
for many of your faults.

Be full of love for others,
following the example of Christ
who loved you and gave himself to
God as a sacrifice to take away
your sins.

TODAY

_____

_____

_____

Romans 5:5.   1 John 4:19, 16.   1 Peter 4:8.   Ephesians 5:2.

Don't say,
"Now I can pay him back
for all his meanness to me!"

Practice loving each other, for
love comes from God and those
who are loving and kind show that
they are the children of God,
and that they are getting to know
him better. But if a person isn't
loving and kind, it shows that he
doesn't know God—for God is love.

God showed how much he
loved us by sending his only Son
into this wicked world to bring
to us eternal life through his death.
In this act we see what real love
is: it is not our love for God, but
his love for us when he sent his
Son to satisfy God's anger against
our sins.

Since God loved us as much as
that, we surely ought to love
each other too.

TODAY _____

_____

_____

Proverbs 24:29.   1 John 4:7, 8, 9, 10, 11.

If you are friendly only to your friends, how are you different from anyone else?

Give a warm welcome to any
[one] who wants to join you,
even though his faith is weak.
Don't criticize him for having
different ideas from yours about
what is right and wrong.

Work happily together. Don't try
to act big.

When others are happy, be happy
with them. If they are sad, share
their sorrow.

TODAY _____

_____

_____

Matthew 5:47. Romans 14:1. Romans 12:16, 15.

**God has chosen
poor people
to be rich in faith,
and the Kingdom of Heaven is theirs,
for that is the gift God has promised
to all those who love him.**

If a man comes into your church dressed in expensive clothes and with valuable gold rings on his fingers, and at the same moment another man comes in who is poor and dressed in threadbare clothes, and you make a lot of fuss over the rich man and give him the best seat in the house and say to the poor man, "You can stand over there if you like, or else sit on the floor"—well, judging a man by his wealth shows that you are guided by wrong motives.

How can you claim that you belong to the Lord Jesus Christ, the Lord of glory, if you show favoritism to rich people and look down on poor people?

TODAY _____

_____

_____

James 2:5. James 2:2, 3, 4, 1.

God is both kind and severe.

He is very hard on those who disobey, but very good to you if you continue to love and trust him.

O Jehovah, come and bless us! How long will you delay? Turn away your anger from us. Satisfy us in our earliest youth with your lovingkindness, giving us constant joy to the end of our lives.

Teach us to number our days and recognize how few they are; help us to spend them as we should.

TODAY _____

_____

_____

Romans 11:22.   Psalm 90:13, 14, 12.

SEPTEMBER

The Lord is coming soon.

In that day the wolf and the lamb will lie down together, and the leopard and goats will be at peace. Calves and fat cattle will be safe among lions, and a little child shall lead them all.

The cows will graze among bears; cubs and calves will lie down together, and lions will eat grass like the cows.

Babies will crawl safely among poisonous snakes, and a little child who puts his hand in a nest of deadly adders will pull it out unharmed.

TODAY _____

_____

Philippians 4:5. Isaiah 11:6, 7, 8.

Our natural lives will fade as grass does when it becomes all brown and dry. All our greatness is like a flower that droops and falls; but the Word of the Lord will last forever.

Whatever God says to us is full of living power: it is sharper than the sharpest dagger, cutting swift and deep into our innermost thoughts and desires with all their parts, exposing us for what we really are.

The whole Bible was given to us by inspiration from God and is useful to teach us what is true and to make us realize what is wrong in our lives; it straightens us out and helps us do what is right.

Know what [God's] Word says and means.

TODAY _____

_____

2 Timothy 2:15.   1 Peter 1:24, 25.   Hebrews 4:12.   2 Timothy 3:16.

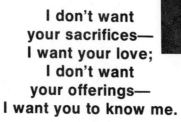

**I don't want
your sacrifices—
I want your love;
I don't want
your offerings—
I want you to know me.**

Learn the meaning of this verse
of Scripture, "It isn't your
sacrifices and your gifts I want—I
want you to be merciful." For I
have come to urge sinners, not the
self-righteous, back to God.

Oh, that we might know the
Lord! Let us press on to know
him, and he will respond to us as
surely as the coming of dawn or
the rain of early spring.

Happy are those who long to
be just and good, for they shall be
completely satisfied.

TODAY _____

_____

_____

Hosea 6:6.   Matthew 9:13.   Hosea 6:3.   Matthew 5:6.

**A person
who is pure of heart
sees goodness and purity
in everything.**

But a person whose own heart is evil and untrusting finds evil in everything, for his dirty mind and rebellious heart color all he sees and hears.

Such persons claim they know God, but from seeing the way they act, one knows they don't. They are rotten and disobedient, worthless so far as doing anything good is concerned.

But as for you, speak up for the right living that goes along with true Christianity.

TODAY _____

_____

_____

Titus 1:15a. Titus 1:15b, 16. Titus 2:1.

SEPTEMBER

**Learn to put aside
your own desires
so that you will become
patient and godly,
gladly letting God
have his way with you.**

This will make possible the next step, which is for you to enjoy other people and to like them, and finally you will grow to love them deeply. The more you go on in this way, the more you will grow strong spiritually and become fruitful and useful to our Lord Jesus Christ.

Work hard to prove that you really are among those God has called and chosen, and then you will never stumble or fall away. And God will open wide the gates of heaven for you to enter into the eternal kingdom of our Lord and Savior Jesus Christ.

TODAY _____

_____

2 Peter 1:6. 2 Peter 1:7, 8, 10, 11.

**Don't let
the excitement
of being young
cause you to forget
about your Creator.
Honor him in your youth.**

It will be too late . . . to try to remember him, when the sun and light and moon and stars are dim to your old eyes, and there is no silver lining left among your clouds. For there will come a time when your limbs will tremble with age, and your strong legs will become weak, and your teeth will be too few to do their work, and there will be blindness, too.

And you will waken at dawn with the first note of the birds; but you yourself will be deaf and tuneless, with quavering voice.

Yes, remember your Creator now while you are young.

_____ **TODAY**

_____

Ecclesiastes 12:1.   Ecclesiastes 12:2, 3, 4, 6.

SEPTEMBER

**Now is the time
to seek the Lord,
that he may come
and shower salvation
upon you.**

Come to the Lord and say, "O Lord, take away our sins; be gracious to us and receive us."

There is salvation in no one else! Under all heaven there is no other name for men to call upon to save them.

And we all can be saved in this same way, by coming to Christ, no matter who we are or what we have been like.

We are saved by faith in Christ and not by the good things we do.

TODAY _____

_____

_____

Hosea 10:12. Hosea 14:2. Acts 4:12. Romans 3:22, 28.

**The disciples
came to Jesus
to ask which of them
would be greatest
in the Kingdom of Heaven!**

Jesus called a small child over
to him and set the little fellow
down among them, and said,
"Unless you turn to God from
your sins and become as little
children, you will never get into
the Kingdom of Heaven. Therefore
anyone who humbles himself as
this little child, is the greatest in
the Kingdom of Heaven.

"Don't look down upon a single
one of these little children. For I
tell you that in heaven their angels
have constant access to my Father."

TODAY _____

_____

_____

Matthew 18:1. Matthew 18:2, 3, 4, 10.

Peacemakers . . .
plant seeds of peace
and reap a harvest
of goodness.

Let us follow the Holy Spirit's
leading in every part of our lives.
Then we won't need to look for
honors and popularity, which
lead to jealousy and hard feelings.

Cling tightly to your faith in
Christ and always keep your
conscience clear, doing what you
know is right.

TODAY _____

_____

James 3:18.   Galatians 5:25, 26.   1 Timothy 1:19.

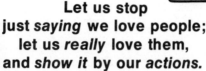

Let us stop just *saying* we love people; let us *really* love them, and *show it* by our *actions*.

Then we will know for sure, by our actions, that we are on God's side, and our consciences will be clear, even when we stand before the Lord. But if we have bad consciences and feel that we have done wrong, the Lord will surely feel it even more, for he knows everything we do.

If our consciences are clear, we can come to the Lord with perfect assurance and trust, and get whatever we ask for because we are obeying him and doing the things that please him.

And this is what God says we must do: Believe on the name of his Son Jesus Christ, and love one another.

TODAY _____

_____

_____

1 John 3:18.   1 John 3:19, 20, 21, 22, 23.

SEPTEMBER

A beautiful young girl named Rebekah arrived with a water jug on her shoulder and filled it at the spring. Running over to her, the servant asked her for a drink.

"Certainly, sir," she said, and quickly lowered the jug for him to drink. Then she said, "I'll draw water for your camels, too, until they have enough!"

So she emptied the jug into the watering trough and ran down to the spring again and kept carrying water to the camels until they had enough. Then at last, when the camels had finished drinking, he produced a quarter-ounce gold earring and two five-ounce golden bracelets for her wrists.

Work hard and cheerfully at all you do, just as though you were working for the Lord. If you give, you will get!

TODAY _____

_____

_____

Luke 6:38. Genesis 24:15, 16, 17, 18, 19, 20, 22. Colossians 3:23. Luke 6:38.

Whatever measure
you use to give—
large or small—
will be used
to measure
what is given
back to you.

A soft answer turns away wrath, but harsh words cause quarrels.

YOU THINK YOU'RE SMART, CHARLIE BROWN...

WELL, YOU'RE **NOT**! NYAAH!

© 1967 United Feature Syndicate, Inc.

Don't get involved in foolish arguments which only upset people and make them angry. God's people must not be quarrelsome; they must be gentle, patient teachers of those who are wrong.

Don't quarrel with anyone. Be at peace with everyone, just as much as possible.

If you are slapped on one cheek, turn the other too.

There is a saying, "Love your *friends* and hate your enemies." But I [Jesus] say: Love your *enemies*! Pray for those who *persecute* you! In that way you will be acting as true sons of your Father in heaven.

TODAY _____

_____

Proverbs 15:1.   2 Timothy 2:23, 24.   Romans 12:18.   Matthew 5:39, 43, 44, 45.

**Jealousy
is more dangerous
and cruel than anger.**

Don't brag about being wise and good
if you are bitter and jealous and selfish;
that is the worst sort of lie. For jealousy
and selfishness are not God's kind of
wisdom. Such things are earthly,
unspiritual, inspired by the devil. For
wherever there is jealousy or selfish
ambition, there will be disorder and
every other kind of evil.

But the wisdom that comes from
heaven is first of all pure and full of
quiet gentleness. Then it is peace loving
and courteous. It . . . is willing to yield
to others; it is full of mercy and good deeds.

And those who are peacemakers will
plant seeds of peace and reap a harvest
of goodness.

TODAY

Proverbs 27:4. James 3:14, 15, 16, 17, 18.

Be just and fair to all, the Lord God says. Do what's right and good.

Usually no one will hurt you for wanting to do good. But even if they should, you are to be envied, for God will reward you for it. Quietly trust yourself to Christ your Lord and if anybody asks why you believe as you do, be ready to tell him, and do it in a gentle and respectful way.

Do what is right; then if men speak against you, calling you evil names, they will become ashamed of themselves for falsely accusing you when you have only done what is good. Remember, if God wants you to suffer, it is better to suffer for doing good than for doing wrong!

TODAY _____

_____

_____

Isaiah 56:1. 1 Peter 3:13, 14, 15, 16, 17.

OCTOBER

2

Live clean, innocent lives.

If someone mistreats you because you are a Christian, don't curse him; pray that God will bless him.

Don't say, "Now I can pay him back for all his meanness to me!"

Stay away from complaining and arguing, so that no one can speak a word of blame against you.

Practice loving each other.

_____ TODAY

_____

_____

Philippians 2:15. Romans 12:14. Proverbs 24:29. Philippians 2:14, 15. 1 John 4:7.

A wise man controls his temper.

The Lord descended in the form of a pillar of cloud and stood there with him, and passed in front of him and announced the meaning of his name. "I am Jehovah, the merciful and gracious God," he said, "slow to anger and rich in steadfast love and truth."

Follow God's example in everything you do just as a much loved child imitates his father.

When the Holy Spirit controls our lives he will produce this kind of fruit in us: love, joy, peace, patience, kindness, goodness, faithfulness, gentleness and self-control.

Don't let the sun go down with you still angry—get over it quickly; for when you are angry you give a mighty foothold to the devil.

TODAY

_____

_____

Proverbs 14:29. Exodus 34:5, 6. Ephesians 5:1. Galatians 5:22, 23. Ephesians 4:26.

**Though once your heart
was full of darkness,
now it is full of light from the Lord,
and your behavior should show it!**

Because of this light within you,
you should do only what is good
and right and true.
Learn as you go along what
pleases the Lord. Take no part in
the worthless pleasures of evil
and darkness, but instead, rebuke
and expose them. When you
expose them, the light shines in
upon their sin and shows it up,
and when they see how wrong they
really are, some of them may
even become children of light!

TODAY _____

_____

_____

Ephesians 5:8.   Ephesians 5:9, 10, 11, 13.

Don't tell lies
to each other.

It was your old life with all its
wickedness that did that sort of
thing; now it is dead and gone.
You are living a brand new kind
of life that is continually learning
more and more of what is right,
and trying constantly to be more
and more like Christ who created
this new life within you.

Since you have been chosen
by God who has given you this
new kind of life, and because of
his deep love and concern for you,
you should practice tenderhearted
mercy and kindness to others.

TODAY _____

_____

_____

Colossians 3:9a.   Colossians 3:9b, 10, 12.

Without a bit and bridle a horse is difficult to control.

If anyone can control his tongue, it proves that he has perfect control over himself in every other way.

We can make a large horse turn around and go wherever we want by means of a small bit in his mouth. And a tiny rudder makes a huge ship turn wherever the pilot wants it to go, even though the winds are strong.

So also the tongue is a small thing, but what enormous damage it can do. A great forest can be set on fire by one tiny spark. And the tongue is a flame of fire. It

is full of wickedness, and poisons
every part of the body. And the
tongue is set on fire by hell itself,
and can turn our whole lives into
a blazing flame of destruction and
disaster.

_____ **TODAY**

_____

_____

James 3:2, 3, 4, 5, 6.

OCTOBER

7

My problems go from bad to worse.

The Lord will work out his plans
for my life—for your
lovingkindness, Lord, continues
forever. Don't abandon me—for
you made me.

How precious it is, Lord, to
realize that you are thinking about
me constantly! I can't even count
how many times a day your
thoughts turn towards me. And
when I waken in the morning, you
are still thinking of me!

Search me, O God, and know my
heart; test my thoughts. Point
out anything you find in me that
makes you sad, and lead me
along the path of everlasting life.

TODAY _____

_____

Psalm 25:17. Psalm 138:8. Psalm 139:17, 18, 23, 24.

**Happy is the man
who doesn't give in
and do wrong
when he is tempted.**

For afterwards he will get as his
reward the crown of life that
God has promised those who love
him. And remember, when
someone wants to do wrong it is
never God who is tempting him,
for God never wants to do wrong
and never tempts anyone else to
do it. Temptation is the pull of
man's own evil thoughts and
wishes. These evil thoughts lead to
evil actions and afterwards to the
death penalty from God. So don't
be misled.

But whatever is good and perfect
comes to us from God, the
Creator of all light, and he shines
forever without change or shadow.

_____ **TODAY**

_____

James 1:12a.   James 1:12b, 13, 14, 15, 16, 17.

OCTOBER

9

Who is the greatest liar?

The one who says that Jesus is not Christ. Such a person is antichrist, for he does not believe in God the Father and in his Son.

Watch out for the false leaders—and there are many of them around—who don't believe that Jesus Christ came to earth as a human being with a body like ours.

Beware of being like them . . . See to it that you win your full reward from the Lord.

Do not let this happy trust in the Lord die away . . . Remember your reward!

TODAY _____

_____

_____

1 John 2:22.   2 John 7, 8.   Hebrews 10:35.

God loved the world so much that he gave his only Son.

Anyone who believes in him shall not perish but have eternal life.

Those who don't trust him have already been tried and condemned for not believing in the only Son of God. Their sentence is based on this fact: that the Light from heaven came into the world, but they loved the darkness more than the Light, for their deeds were evil.

But those doing right come gladly to the Light to let everyone see that they are doing what God wants them to.

TODAY _____

_____

_____

John 3:16a. John 3:16b, 18, 19, 21.

Lord, you are my light!

We can be mirrors
that brightly reflect the glory of
the Lord. And as the Spirit of the
Lord works within us, we
become more and more like him.

For from the very beginning
God decided that those who came
to him . . . should become like
his Son. And having chosen us, he
called us to come to him; and
when we came, he declared us
"not guilty," filled us with
Christ's goodness, gave us right
standing with himself, and
promised us his glory.

So become more and more in
every way like Christ.

_____ **TODAY**

_____

_____

2 Samuel 22:29.   2 Corinthians 3:18.   Romans 8:29, 30.   Ephesians 4:16.

OCTOBER

12

**Your attitudes
and thoughts
must all be
constantly changing
for the better.**

Don't copy the behavior and customs of this world, but be a new and different person with a fresh newness in all you do and think.

You are living a brand new kind of life that is continually learning more and more of what is right, and trying constantly to be more and more like Christ who created this new life within you.

Yes, you must be a new and different person, holy and good. Clothe yourself with this new nature.

TODAY _____

_____

_____

Ephesians 4:23. Romans 12:2. Colossians 3:10. Ephesians 4:24.

Don't grumble about each other.

Get rid of your feelings of hatred. Don't just pretend to be good! Be done with dishonesty and jealousy and talking about others behind their backs. Now that you realize how kind the Lord has been to you, put away all evil, deception, envy, and fraud. Long to grow up into the fullness of your salvation; cry for this as a baby cries for his milk.

Come to Christ, who is the living Foundation of Rock upon which God builds; though men have spurned him, he is very precious to God who has chosen him above all others.

_____ **TODAY**

_____

_____

James 5:9. 1 Peter 2:1, 2, 3, 4.

At the name of Jesus every knee shall bow in heaven and on earth and under the earth.

Every tongue shall confess that Jesus Christ is Lord, to the glory of God the Father.

Kings along the Mediterranean coast—the kings of Tarshish and the islands—and those from Sheba and from Seba—all will bring their gifts. Yes, kings from everywhere! All will bow before him! All will serve him!

The world is his throne.

His power is incredible.

_____ **TODAY**

_____

_____

Philippians 2:10. Philippians 2:11. Psalm 72:10, 11. Psalm 93:1. Nahum 1:3.

Bartimaeus heard that Jesus from Nazareth was near.

He began to shout out, "Jesus, Son of David, have mercy on me!"

When Jesus heard him he stopped there in the road and said, "Tell him to come here."

So they called the blind man. "You lucky fellow," they said, "come on, he's calling you!" Bartimaeus yanked off his old coat and flung it aside, jumped up and came to Jesus.

"O Teacher," the blind man said, "I want to see!"

And Jesus said to him, "All right, it's done. Your faith has healed you." And instantly the blind man could see, and followed Jesus down the road!

Jesus Christ is the same yesterday, today, and forever.

TODAY _____

_____

_____

Mark 10:47a. Mark 10:47b, 49, 52. Hebrews 13:8.

Even before
I was born
God had chosen me
to be his.

Long ago, even before he made
the world, God chose us to be
his very own, through what Christ
would do for us; he decided
then to make us holy in his eyes,
without a single fault—we who
stand before him covered with his
love. His unchanging plan has
always been to adopt us into his
own family by sending Jesus
Christ to die for us. And he did
this because he wanted to!

It is God himself who has made
us what we are and given us
new lives from Christ Jesus; and
long ages ago he planned that
we should spend these lives in
helping others.

TODAY _____

_____

_____

Galatians 1:15. Ephesians 1:4, 5. Ephesians 2:10.

OCTOBER

17

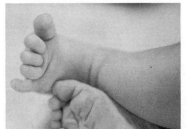

**You made
my body, Lord;
now give
me sense
to heed
your laws.**

Keep me far from every wrong;
help me, undeserving as I am, to
obey your laws, for I have chosen
to do right. I cling to your
commands and follow them as
closely as I can. Lord, don't let
me make a mess of things. If you
will only help me to want your
will, then I will follow your laws
even more closely.

Just tell me what to do and I will
do it, Lord. As long as I live I'll
wholeheartedly obey. Make me walk
along the right paths for I know
how delightful they really are.

_____ **TODAY**

_____

_____

Psalm 119:73.   Psalm 119:29, 30, 31, 32, 33, 34, 35.

Honey whets the appetite, and so does wisdom!

When you enjoy becoming wise, there is hope for you! A bright future lies ahead!

Yes, if you want better insight and discernment, and are searching for them as you would for lost money or hidden treasure, then wisdom will be given you, and knowledge of God himself; you will soon learn the importance of reverence for the Lord and of trusting him.

For the Lord grants wisdom! His every word is a treasure of knowledge and understanding.

TODAY _____

_____

_____

Proverbs 24:13a.   Proverbs 24:13b, 14.   Proverbs 2:3, 4, 5, 6.

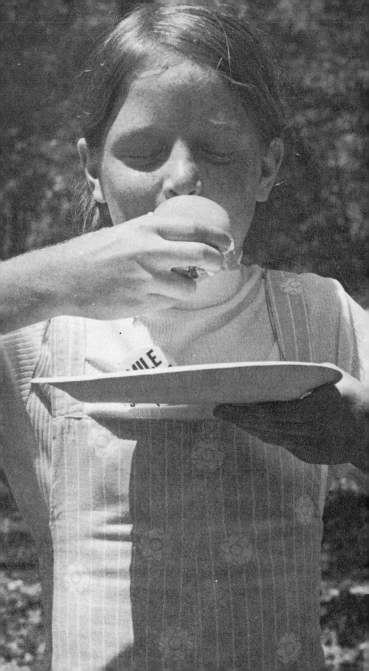

OCTOBER

19

What a wonderful God he is!

There is none like the God
   of Jerusalem—
he descends from the
   heavens in majestic splendor
   to help you.
The eternal God is your
   Refuge,
and underneath are the
   everlasting arms.

His brilliant splendor fills the
   earth and sky;
his glory fills the heavens,
   and the earth is full of his praise!

What a wonderful God he is!

TODAY _____

_____

_____

Habakkuk 3:3. Deuteronomy 33:26, 27. Habakkuk 3:3.

OCTOBER 20

The Lord is coming soon.

Rejoice greatly, O my people! Shout with joy! For look—your King is coming! He is the Righteous One, the Victor!

The Lord . . . will save his people in that day, as a Shepherd caring for his sheep. They shall shine in his land as glittering jewels in a crown. How wonderful and beautiful all shall be!

The abundance of grain and wine will make the young men and girls flourish; they will be radiant with health and happiness.

_____ **TODAY**

_____

_____

Philippians 4:5.   Zechariah 9:9, 16, 17.

21

**Never be afraid
to tell others
about our Lord.**

If anybody asks why you believe and
as you do, be ready to tell him,
do it in a gentle and respectful way.

You are to go into all the world
and preach the Good News to
everyone, everywhere.

It is God's powerful method of
bringing all who believe it to heaven.

As you share your faith with
others it will grip their lives too,
as they see the wealth of good
things in you that come from
Christ Jesus.

TODAY _____

_____

_____

2 Timothy 1:8.   1 Peter 3:15.   Mark 16:15.   Romans 1:16.   Philemon 6.

"Quick! Mix up some pancakes!"

Abraham . . . suddenly noticed
three men coming toward him.
He sprang up and ran to meet
them and welcomed them.

"Sirs," he said, "please don't go
any further. Stop awhile and rest
here in the shade of this tree while
I get water to refresh your feet,
and a bite to eat to strengthen you."

Then Abraham ran back to the
tent and said to Sarah, "Quick! Mix
up some pancakes!"

Don't forget to be kind to
strangers, for some who have
done this have entertained angels
without realizing it!

TODAY _____

_____

_____

Genesis 18:6.   Genesis 18:2, 3, 4, 5, 6.   Hebrews 13:2.

OCTOBER

23

Be wise
and stay
in God's paths

We are not our own bosses to
live or die as we ourselves might
choose.

I advise you to obey only the
Holy Spirit's instructions. He will
tell you where to go and what to
do, and then you won't always be
doing the wrong things your evil
nature wants you to.

For we naturally love to do evil
things that are just the opposite
from the things that the Holy
Spirit tells us to do.

God . . . will show you how to
escape temptation's power so that
you can bear up patiently against it.

TODAY _____

_____

_____

Proverbs 23:19.   Romans 14:7.   Galatians 6:16, 17.   1 Corinthians 10:13.

OCTOBER

24

**The
wrong
desires
that come
into your life
aren't anything
new and different.**

Jesus was led out into the
wilderness by the Holy Spirit, to
be tempted there by Satan.

You can trust God to keep the
temptation from becoming so
strong that you can't stand up
against it, for he has promised this
and will do what he says.

For since he himself has now
been through suffering and
temptation, he knows what it is like
when we suffer and are tempted,
and he is wonderfully able to help us.

TODAY _____

_____

_____

1 Corinthians 10:13.   Matthew 4:1.   1 Corinthians 10:13.   Hebrews 2:18.

The Most High God . . . does whatever he thinks best.

When God saw that they [the people of Nineveh] had put a stop to their evil ways, he abandoned his plan to destroy them, and didn't carry it through.

This change of plans made Jonah very angry.

Woe to the man who fights with his Creator. Does the pot argue with its maker? Does the clay dispute with him who forms it, saying, "Stop, you're doing it wrong!" or the pot exclaim, "How clumsy can you be!"?

_____ **TODAY**

_____

_____

Daniel 4:34, 35. Jonah 3:10. Jonah 4:1. Isaiah 45:9.

**Don't talk so much.
You keep putting
your foot in your mouth.
Be sensible and
turn off the flow!**

Don't ever forget that it is best
to listen much, speak little, and
not become angry.

It is better to be slow-tempered
than famous; it is better to have
self-control than to control an
army.

If anyone can control his
tongue, it proves that he has
perfect control over himself in
every other way.

Help me, Lord, to keep my
mouth shut and my lips sealed.

TODAY _____

_____

_____

Proverbs 10:19. James 1:19. Proverbs 16:32. James 3:2. Psalm 141:3.

OCTOBER

27

**I know everything
about you.
I know all your plans
and where
you are going next.**

You chart the path ahead of me,
and tell me where to stop and
rest. Every moment, you know
where I am. You know what I am
going to say before I even say it.

2 Kings 19:27.   Psalm 139:3, 4, 8, 9, 10.

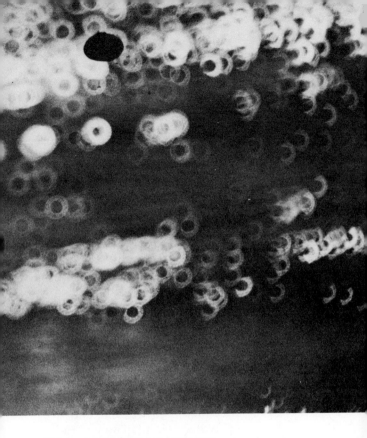

If I go up to heaven, you are there; if I go down to the place of the dead, you are there. If I ride the morning winds to the farthest oceans, even there your hand will guide me, your strength will support me.

_____ **TODAY**

_____

OCTOBER

28

**God of gods,
Ruler of kings.**

Blessed be the name of God forever and ever, for he alone has all wisdom and all power. World events are under his control. He removes kings and sets others on their thrones. He gives wise men their wisdom, and scholars their intelligence. He reveals profound mysteries beyond man's understanding. He knows all hidden things, for he is light, and darkness is no obstacle to him.

TODAY _____

_____

_____

Daniel 2:47. Daniel 2:20, 21, 22.

OCTOBER

29

**I am
the Almighty;
obey me
and live
as you should.**

Grow in spiritual strength and become better acquainted with our Lord and Savior Jesus Christ.

We can be mirrors that brightly reflect the glory of the Lord. And as the Spirit of the Lord works within us, we become more and more like him.

As we live with Christ, our love grows more perfect and complete; so we . . . can face him with confidence and joy, because he loves us and we love him too.

_____ **TODAY**

_____

_____

Genesis 17:1.   2 Peter 3:18.   2 Corinthians 3:18.   1 John 4:17.

OCTOBER
30

Now about prayer.

When you pray, don't be like the hypocrites who pretend piety by praying publicly on street corners and in the synagogues where everyone can see them. Truly, that is all the reward they will ever get.

But when you pray, go away by yourself, all alone, and shut the door behind you and pray to your Father secretly, and your Father, who knows your secrets, will reward you.

TODAY _____

_____

_____

Matthew 6:5a.   Matthew 6:5b, 6.

**The
Pharisees . . .
rejected
God's plan
for them.**

"What can I say about such men?"
Jesus asked. "With what shall
I compare them? They are like
a group of children who complain
to their friends, 'You don't
like it if we play "wedding" and
you don't like it if we play "funeral" '!

   "John the Baptist used to go
without food . . . and [the
Pharisees] said, 'He must be
crazy!' But I eat my food . . .
and [the Pharisees] say, 'What a
glutton Jesus is!' "

   "I have come to urge sinners, not
the self-righteous, back to God."

_____ **TODAY**

_____

_____

Luke 7:30.   Luke 7:31, 32, 33, 34.   Matthew 9:13.

**If we say
that we have no sin,
we are only fooling
ourselves.**

All have sinned; all fall short of God's glorious ideal; yet now God declares us "not guilty" of offending him if we trust in Jesus Christ, who in his kindness freely takes away our sins. For God sent Christ Jesus to take the punishment for our sins and to end all God's anger against us. He used Christ's blood and our faith as the means of saving us from his wrath.

For God loved the world so much that he gave his only Son so that anyone who believes in him shall not perish but have eternal life.

TODAY _____

_____

_____

1 John 1:8.   Romans 3:23, 24, 25.   John 3:16.

NOVEMBER

**The Lord
still waits
for you
to come to him,
so he can
show you his love.**

"Come, let's talk this over!" says the Lord; "no matter how deep the stain of your sins, I can take it out and make you as clean as freshly fallen snow. Even if you are stained as red as crimson, I can make you white as wool."

You belong to Christ Jesus, and though you once were far away from God, now you have been brought very near to him because of what Jesus Christ has done for you with his blood.

TODAY _____

_____

_____

Isaiah 30:18. Isaiah 1:18. Ephesians 2:13.

NOVEMBER

3

Don't be anxious about tomorrow.

God will take care of your tomorrow too. Live one day at a time.

Trust the Lord completely; don't ever trust yourself. In everything you do, put God first, and he will direct you and crown your efforts with success.

Let him have all your worries and cares, for he is always thinking about you and watching everything that concerns you.

_____ **TODAY**

_____

_____

Matthew 6:34. Proverbs 3:5, 6. 1 Peter 5:7.

**The Lord
is good.
When
trouble
comes,
he is
the place
to go!**

And so we need not fear even if
the world blows up, and the
mountains crumble into the sea.

He shows his power in the
terrors of the cyclone and the
raging storms; clouds are
billowing dust beneath his feet!

In his presence mountains
quake and hills melt.

The Lord saves the godly! He
is their salvation and their refuge
when trouble comes.

TODAY _____

_____

_____

Nahum 1:7.   Psalm 46:2.   Nahum 1:3, 5.   Psalm 37:39.

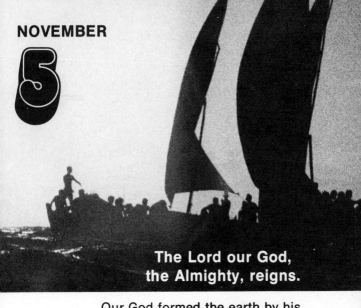

NOVEMBER

5

The Lord our God, the Almighty, reigns.

Our God formed the earth by his power and wisdom, and by his intelligence he hung the stars in space and stretched out the heavens.

It is his voice that echoes in the thunder of the storm clouds. He causes mist to rise upon the earth; he sends the lightning and brings the rain, and from his treasuries he brings the wind.

O Lord, there is no other god like you. For you are great and your name is full of power.

TODAY _____

_____

_____

Revelation 19:6.   Jeremiah 10:12, 13, 6.

The sailors sailing the seven seas . . . they, too, observe the power of God in action.

He calls to the storm winds; the waves rise high. Their ships are tossed to the heavens and sink again to the depths; the sailors cringe in terror. They reel and stagger like drunkards and are at their wit's end.

Then they cry to the Lord in their trouble, and he saves them. He calms the storm and stills the waves.

What a blessing is that stillness, as he brings them safely into harbor!

_____ **TODAY**

_____

_____

Psalm 107:23, 24.   Psalm 107:25, 26, 27, 28, 29, 30.

The Lord delights in you.

Can a mother forget her little child and not have love for her own son? Yet even if that should be, I will not forget you.

The steps of good men are directed by the Lord. He delights in each step they take.

His joy is in those who reverence him, those who expect him to be loving and kind.

"They shall be mine," says the Lord of Hosts, "in that day when I make up my jewels."

_____ **TODAY**

_____

_____

Isaiah 62:4. Isaiah 49:15. Psalm 37:23. Psalm 147:11. Malachi 3:17.

The Lord is coming soon.

Those who feared and loved the Lord spoke often of him to each other. And he had a Book of Remembrance drawn up in which he recorded the names of those who feared him and loved to think about him.

"They shall be mine," says the Lord of Hosts, "in that day when I make up my jewels."

You will go free, leaping with joy like calves let out to pasture.

TODAY _____

_____

_____

Philippians 4:5. Malachi 3:16, 17. Malachi 4:2.

NOVEMBER

**In a race,
everyone runs
but only one person
gets first prize.**

To win the contest you must
deny yourselves many things that
would keep you from doing your
best. An athlete goes to all this
trouble just to win a blue ribbon or
a silver cup, but we do it for a
heavenly reward that never
disappears.

Let us strip off anything that
slows us down or holds us back,
and especially those sins that wrap
themselves so tightly around our
feet and trip us up; and let us run
with patience the particular race
that God has set before us.

Keep your eyes on Jesus, our
leader and instructor.

_____ **TODAY**

_____

_____

1 Corinthians 9:24. 1 Corinthians 9:25. Hebrews 12:1, 2.

NOVEMBER

10

What a God he is!
How perfect
in every way!

He made the world and everything in it, and since he is Lord of heaven and earth, he doesn't live in man-made temples; and human hands can't minister to his needs—for he has no needs! He himself gives life and breath to everything, and satisfies every need there is.

He is not far from any one of us. For in him we live and move and are!

_____ **TODAY**

_____

_____

Psalm 18:30. Acts 17:24, 25, 27, 28.

NOVEMBER

11

Even my best friend has turned against me.

A messenger soon arrived in Jerusalem to tell King David, "All Israel has joined Absalom in a conspiracy against you!"

On every side I [Jeremiah] hear their whispered threats, and am afraid. "We will report you," they say. Even those who were my friends are watching me.

But God is my helper. He is a friend of mine! The Lord stands beside me like a great warrior.

TODAY _____

_____

Psalm 41:9. 2 Samuel 15:13. Jeremiah 20:10. Psalm 54:4. Jeremiah 20:11.

Love your *enemies*. Do *good* to those who *hate* you.

Pray for the happiness of those who *curse* you; implore God's blessing on those who *hurt* you.

If someone slaps you on one cheek, let him slap the other too! If someone demands your coat, give him your shirt besides. Give what you have to anyone who asks you for it; and when things are taken away from you, don't worry about getting them back. Treat others as you want them to treat you.

TODAY _____

_____

_____

Luke 6:27. Luke 6:28, 29, 30, 31.

NOVEMBER

Stay out of all quarrels.

Jehovah is kind and merciful, slow to get angry, full of love.

Follow God's example in everything you do. Be full of love for others, following the example of Christ who loved you.

Be . . . tenderhearted, forgiving one another, just as God has forgiven you because you belong to Christ.

You can have real love for everyone because your souls have been cleansed from selfishness and hatred when you trusted Christ to save you; so see to it that you really do love each other warmly, with all your hearts.

TODAY _____

_____

_____

Hebrews 12:14.   Psalm 145:8.   Ephesians 5:1, 2.   Ephesians 4:32.   1 Peter 1:22.

I have loved you
even as the Father has loved me.
Live within my love.

When you obey me you are
living in my love, just as I obey
my Father and live in his love. I
have told you this so that you
will be filled with my joy. Yes, your
cup of joy will overflow.

I demand that you love each
other as much as I love you.
And here is how to measure it—the
greatest love is shown when a
person lays down his life for his
friends.

TODAY _____

_____

_____

John 15:9.   John 15:10, 11, 12, 13.

NOVEMBER 15

**The day
one dies
is better
than the day
he is born!**

Living means opportunities for Christ,
and dying—well, that's better yet.

Sometimes I want to live and
at other times I don't, for I long to
go and be with Christ. How much
happier for *me* than being here!

We look forward with confidence
to our heavenly bodies, realizing
that every moment we spend in
these earthly bodies is time
spent away from our eternal home
in heaven with Jesus.

TODAY _____

_____

Ecclesiastes 7:1.   Philippians 1:21, 23.   2 Corinthians 5:6.

**O God,
my heart
is ready
to praise you!**

I will praise you everywhere
around the world, in every
nation. For your lovingkindness is
great beyond measure, high as
the heavens. Your faithfulness
reaches the skies. His glory is far
more vast than the heavens. It
towers above the earth.

_____ **TODAY**

_____

_____

Psalm 108:1. Psalm 108:3, 4, 5.

What God in all of heaven or earth can do what you have done for us?

Who in all of heaven can be compared with God? What mightiest angel is anything like him? O Jehovah, Commander of the heavenly armies, where is there any other Mighty One like you? Faithfulness is your very character.

All heaven shall praise your miracles, O Lord; myriads of angels will praise you for your faithfulness.

_____ **TODAY**

_____

_____

Deuteronomy 3:24.   Psalm 89:6, 8, 5.

NOVEMBER 18

He gave
his only Son.

Since earliest times men have seen the earth and sky and all God made, and have known of his existence and great eternal power.

Day and night they keep on telling about God. Without a sound or word, silent in the skies, their message reaches out to all the world.

When I look up into the night skies and see the work of your fingers—the moon and the stars you have made—I cannot understand how you can bother with mere puny man, to pay any attention to him!

When Adam sinned, sin entered the entire human race. His sin spread death throughout all the world.

God loved the world so much that he gave his only Son so that anyone who believes in him shall not perish but have eternal life.

TODAY _____

_____

John 3:16.   Romans 1:20.   Psalm 19:2, 3.   Psalm 8:3, 4.
Romans 5:12.   John 3:16.

Abraham *believed* God.

That is why God canceled his sins and declared him "not guilty."

But didn't he earn his right to heaven by all the good things he did? No, for being saved is a gift; if a person could earn it by being good, then it wouldn't be free—but it is! It is *given* to those who do *not* work for it. For God declares sinners to be good in his sight if they have faith in Christ to save them from God's wrath.

King David spoke of this, describing the happiness of an undeserving sinner who is declared "not guilty" by God. "Blessed, and to be envied," he said, "are those whose sins are forgiven and put out of sight."

TODAY _____

_____

Romans 4:3a.   Romans 4:3b, 4, 5, 6, 7.

**God will
accept us . . .
when we believe
the promises
of God.**

When God told Abraham that he would give him a son who would have many descendants and become a great nation, Abraham believed God even though such a promise just couldn't come to pass! And because his faith was strong, he didn't worry about the fact that he was too old to be a father, at the age of one hundred, and that Sarah his wife, at ninety, was also much too old to have a baby.

He was completely sure that God was well able to do anything he promised. And because of Abraham's faith God forgave his sins and declared him "not guilty."

_____ **TODAY**

_____

Romans 4:24.   Romans 4:18, 19, 21, 22.

God made man like his Maker.

We are the sons of God. We shouldn't think of God as an idol made by men from gold or silver or chipped from stone.

God is so rich in mercy; he loved us so much that even though we were spiritually dead and doomed by our sins, he gave us back our lives again when he raised Christ

from the dead. It is God himself who has made us what we are and given us new lives from Christ Jesus; and long ages ago he planned that we should spend these lives in helping others.

TODAY _____

_____

Genesis 1:27.   Acts 17:28, 29.   Ephesians 2:4, 5, 10.

NOVEMBER

You are the world's light . . .
glowing in the night
for all to see.

Live clean, innocent lives as
children of God in a dark world
full of people who are crooked and
stubborn. Shine out among them
like beacon lights, holding out to
them the Word of Life.

Those who are wise—the people
of God—shall shine as brightly
as the sun's brilliance, and those
who turn many to righteousness
will glitter like stars forever.

TODAY _____

_____

_____

Matthew 5:14. Philippians 2:15, 16. Daniel 12:3.

Don't praise yourself; let others do it!

Be honest in your estimate of yourselves, measuring your value by how much faith God has given you.

What do you have that God hasn't given you? And if all you have is from God, why act as though you are so great, and as though you have accomplished something on your own?

For the proud shall be humbled, but the humble shall be honored.

So give yourselves humbly to God. And when you draw close to God, God will draw close to you.

TODAY _____

_____

Proverbs 27:2.   Romans 12:3.   1 Corinthians 4:7.   Luke 18:14.   James 4:7, 8.

NOVEMBER

24

**Students
are wise
who master
what their teachers
tell them.**

For the value of wisdom is far above rubies; nothing can be compared with it. Wisdom and good judgment live together, for wisdom knows where to discover knowledge and understanding.

Leave behind your foolishness and begin to live; learn how to be wise.

Make the hours of your day more profitable and the years of your life more fruitful.

_____ **TODAY**

_____

_____

Ecclesiastes 12:11.   Proverbs 8:11, 12.   Proverbs 9:6, 11.

**Hard work
means prosperity;
only a fool
idles away his time.**

In everything you do, put God
first, and he will direct you and
crown your efforts with success.

Don't be conceited, sure of
your own wisdom. Instead, trust
and reverence the Lord, and turn
your back on evil; when you do
that, then you will be given
renewed health and vitality.

TODAY _____

_____

_____

Proverbs 12:11. Proverbs 3:6, 7, 8.

NOVEMBER

26

**Nothing
you do
for the
Lord
is ever
wasted.**

Just as you trusted Christ to save you, trust him, too, for each day's problems; live in vital union with him. Let your roots grow down into him and draw up nourishment from him. See that you go on growing in the Lord, and become strong and vigorous in the truth you were taught. Let your lives overflow with joy and thanksgiving for all he has done.

TODAY _____

_____

_____

1 Corinthians 15:58. Colossians 2:6, 7.

Be happy.
Grow in Christ.

Do the good things that result
from being saved, obeying God
with deep reverence, shrinking back
from all that might displease
him. For God is at work within you,
helping you want to obey him,
and then helping you do what he
wants.

Be a new and different person
with a fresh newness in all you
do and think. Then you will learn
from your own experience how
his ways will really satisfy you.

TODAY _____

_____

_____

2 Corinthians 13:11.　Philippians 2:12, 13.　Romans 12:2.

Be delighted with the Lord.

Then he will give you all your
heart's desires. Commit
everything you do to the Lord.
Trust him to help you do it and
he will.

   Don't be impatient for the Lord
to act! Keep traveling steadily along
his pathway and in due season
he will honor you with every
blessing.

   For the good man—the
blameless, the upright, the man
of peace—he has a wonderful
future ahead of him. For him
there is a happy ending.

_____ **TODAY**

_____

_____

Psalm 37:4a.   Psalm 37:4b, 5, 34, 37.

NOVEMBER

29

Judging a man by his wealth shows that you are guided by wrong motives.

God has chosen poor people to be rich in faith, and the Kingdom of Heaven is theirs, for that is the gift God has promised to all those who love him.

It is good when you truly obey our Lord's command, "You must love and help your neighbors just as much as you love and take care of yourself."

But you are breaking this law of our Lord's when you favor the rich and fawn over them; it is sin.

TODAY _____

_____

_____

James 2:4.   James 2:5, 8, 9.

Be satisfied
with what you have.

Someone called from the crowd,
"Sir, please tell my brother to
divide my father's estate with me."
   But Jesus replied, "Man, who
made me a judge over you to
decide such things as that?
Beware! Don't always be wishing
for what you don't have. For real
life and real living are not related
to how rich we are."
   Do you want to be truly rich?
You already are if you are happy
and good. After all, we didn't bring
any money with us when we
came into the world, and we can't
carry away a single penny when
we die. So we should be well
satisfied without money if we
have enough food and clothing.

_____ **TODAY**

_____

_____

Hebrews 13:5.   Luke 12:13, 14, 15.   1 Timothy 6:6, 7, 8.

Pray about everything.

Pray morning, noon, and night, pleading aloud with God; and he will hear and answer.

Go away by yourself, all alone, and shut the door behind you . . . pray to your Father secretly, and your Father, who knows your secrets, will reward you.

Daniel . . . went home and knelt down as usual in his upstairs bedroom . . . and prayed three times a day, just as he always had, giving thanks to his God.

The earnest prayer of a righteous man has great power and wonderful results.

TODAY _____

_____

_____

Philippians 4:6.   Psalm 55:17.   Matthew 6:6.   Daniel 6:10.   James 5:16.

DECEMBER

2

What a glorious Lord! He who daily bears our burdens also gives us our salvation.

Some will come to me—those the Father has given me—and I will never, never reject them. For it is my Father's will that everyone who sees his Son and believes on him should have eternal life.

Trust the Lord completely; don't ever trust yourself. In everything you do, put God first, and he will direct you and crown your efforts with success.

TODAY _____

_____

_____

Psalm 68:19.   John 6:37, 40.   Proverbs 3:5, 6.

We have the Lord our God to fight our battles for us!

Happy is the man who has the
God of Jacob as his helper,
whose hope is in the Lord his God.

The eyes of the Lord are
watching over those who fear him,
who rely upon his steady love.
He will keep them from death even
in times of famine!

For God has said, "I will never,
never fail you nor forsake you."
That is why we can say without
any doubt or fear, "The Lord is
my Helper."

_____ **TODAY**

_____

_____

2 Chronicles 32:8. Psalm 146:5. Psalm 33:18, 19. Hebrews 13:5, 6.

**The
godly
man's life
is exciting.**

The steps of good men are
directed by the Lord. He delights
in each step they take. If they fall
it isn't fatal, for the Lord holds
them with his hand.

The good man does not
escape all troubles—he has them
too. But the Lord helps him in
each and every one.

For the Lord watches over all
the plans and paths of godly men,
but the paths of the godless lead
to doom.

_____ **TODAY**

_____

_____

Proverbs 14:14.   Psalm 37:23, 24.   Psalm 34:19.   Psalm 1:6.

DECEMBER

5

Don't worry about *things*— food, drink, and clothes.

For you already have life and a body—and they are far more important than what to eat and wear.

Look at the birds! They don't worry about what to eat—they don't need to sow or reap or store up food—for your heavenly Father feeds them. And you are far more valuable to him than they are.

And why worry about your clothes? Look at the field lilies! They don't worry about theirs. And if God cares so wonderfully for flowers that are here today and gone tomorrow, won't he more surely care for you?

TODAY

_____

_____

_____

Matthew 6:25. Matthew 6:26, 28, 30.

The Lord is good.

When trouble comes, he is the place to go! And he knows everyone who trusts in him!

The Angel of God called to Hagar from the sky, "Hagar, what's wrong? Don't be afraid! For God has heard the lad's cries as he is lying there." Then God opened her eyes and she saw a well; so she refilled the canteen and gave the lad a drink.

He is good to everyone, and his compassion is intertwined with everything he does.

TODAY _____

_____

_____

Nahum 1:7. Genesis 21:17, 19. Psalm 145:9.

DECEMBER

Underneath are the everlasting arms.

When [Peter] looked around at the high waves, he was terrified and began to sink. "Save me, Lord!" he shouted. Instantly Jesus reached out his hand and rescued him. "O man of little faith," Jesus said. "Why did you doubt me?"

The steps of good men are directed by the Lord. He delights in each step they take. If they fall it isn't fatal, for the Lord holds them with his hand.

Let him have all your worries and cares, for he is always thinking about you and watching everything that concerns you.

TODAY _____

_____

_____

Deuteronomy 33:27. Matthew 14:30, 31. Psalm 37:23, 24. 1 Peter 5:7.

**We are
not afraid
. . . to die,
for then
we will be
at home
with the Lord.**

We know that all that happens to
us is working for our good if we
love God and are fitting into his plans.

God will give us our full rights as
his children, including the new
bodies he has promised us—bodies
that will never be sick again and
will never die.

He will wipe away all tears . . .
and there shall be no more death,
nor sorrow, nor crying, nor pain.

_____ **TODAY**

_____

_____

2 Corinthians 5:8.   Romans 8:28, 23.   Revelation 21:4.

Cling tightly
to your faith
in Christ.

DECEMBER

Always keep your conscience clear, doing what you know is right.

Keep away from anything that might take God's place in your hearts.

Worship no other gods, but only Jehovah, for he is a God who claims absolute loyalty and exclusive devotion.

Worship and serve him with a clean heart and a willing mind, for the Lord sees every heart and understands and knows every thought.

TODAY

1 Timothy 1:19. 1 John 5:21. Exodus 34:14. 1 Chronicles 28:9.

DECEMBER

The shark keeps traveling steadily along, spending his entire life searching for food. A shark can live as long as 35 years and during that time he may travel nearly one and a half times around the world—more than 35,000 miles.

I will set my face against anyone who consults mediums and wizards instead of me.

Stay away from idols! I am living and strong! I look after you and care for you. I am like an evergreen tree, yielding my fruit to you throughout the year. My mercies never fail.

Whoever is wise, let him understand these things. Whoever is intelligent, let him listen. For the paths of the Lord are true and right, and good men walk along them. But sinners trying it will fail.

TODAY _____

_____

_____

Leviticus 20:6. Hosea 14:8, 9.

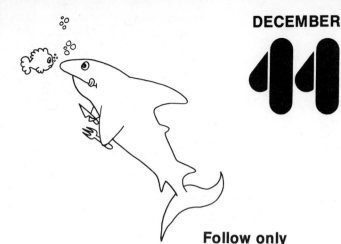

DECEMBER

11

Follow only what is good.

Remember that those who do what is right prove that they are God's children.

Keep traveling steadily along his pathway and in due season he will honor you with every blessing.

For the good man—the blameless, the upright, the man of peace—he has a wonderful future ahead of him. For him there is a happy ending.

TODAY _____

_____

_____

3 John 11. Psalm 37:34, 37.

Jesus of Nazareth . . . went around doing good.

Share each other's troubles and problems, and so obey our Lord's command.

Be humble, thinking of others as better than yourself.

Be kind to each other, tenderhearted, forgiving one another, just as God has forgiven you because you belong to Christ.

Anyone who says he is a Christian should live as Christ did.

TODAY _____

_____

_____

Acts 10:38. Galatians 6:2. Philippians 2:3. Ephesians 4:32. 1 John 2:6.

DECEMBER 13

His Holy Spirit speaks to us deep in our hearts, and tells us that we really are God's children.

And so we should not be like cringing, fearful slaves, but we should behave like God's very own children, adopted into the bosom of his family, and calling to him, "Father, Father."

We are able to hold our heads high no matter what happens and know that all is well, for we know how dearly God loves us.

TODAY _____

_____

_____

Romans 8:16, 15. Romans 5:5.

DECEMBER
14

**Live one day
at a time.**

Because the Lord is my Shepherd, I have everything I need! He lets me rest in the meadow grass and leads me beside the quiet streams.

Let him have all your worries and cares, for he is always thinking about you and watching everything that concerns you.

Commit everything you do to the Lord. Trust him to help you do it and he will.

In everything you do, put God first, and he will direct you and crown your efforts with success.

TODAY _____

_____

_____

Matthew 6:34.   Psalm 23:1, 2.   1 Peter 5:7.   Psalm 37:5.   Proverbs 3:6.

**Don't let anyone
think little of you
because you are young.**

Be a pattern for them in your
love, your faith, and your clean
thoughts.

I would have you learn this
great fact: that a life of doing right
is the wisest life there is. If you
live that kind of life, you'll not limp
or stumble as you run.

For [God] holds our lives in his
hands. And he holds our feet to
the path.

TODAY _____

_____

_____

1 Timothy 4:12.   Proverbs 4:11, 12.   Psalm 66:9.

DECEMBER 16

**The Lord
is great,
and should be
highly praised.**

The Lord made the heavens.
Majesty and honor march
   before him,
Strength and gladness walk
   beside him.
O people of all nations of
   the earth,
Ascribe great strength and
   glory to his name!
Let all the nations say, "It is
   the Lord who reigns."

TODAY _____

_____

_____

1 Chronicles 16:25.   1 Chronicles 16:26, 27, 28, 31.

DECEMBER

O our God, we thank you and praise your glorious name.

Yours is the mighty power and glory and victory and majesty. Everything in the heavens and earth is yours, O Lord, and this is your kingdom. We adore you as being in control of everything.

Riches and honor come from you alone, and you are the Ruler of all mankind; your hand controls power and might, and it is at your discretion that men are made great and given strength.

_____ **TODAY**

_____

_____

1 Chronicles 29:13.   1 Chronicles 29:11, 12.

DECEMBER

[God] alone has all wisdom and all power.

World events are under his control. He removes kings and sets others on their thrones. He gives wise men their wisdom, and scholars their intelligence.

Glory be to God who by his mighty power at work within us is able to do far more than we would ever dare to ask or even dream of—infinitely beyond our highest prayers, desires, thoughts, or hopes.

TODAY _____

_____

_____

_____

Daniel 2:20. Daniel 2:21. Ephesians 3:20.

Marc LeMaire, age 8

It is better to trust the Lord than to put confidence in men.

It is better to take refuge in him than in the mightiest king.

The greatest of men, or the lowest—both alike are nothing in his sight. They weigh less than air on scales.

God has already given you everything you need.

For he holds our lives in his hands. And he holds our feet to the path.

TODAY _____

_____

_____

Psalm 118:8, 9.   Psalm 62:9.   1 Corinthians 3:21.   Psalm 66:9.

God . . . is able
to do far more
than we would ever
dare to ask.

Everything in all the world is his!
All the animals of field and
forest . . . The cattle on a
thousand hills! And all the birds
upon the mountains!
So don't be anxious about
tomorrow. God will take care of
your tomorrow too. Live one day
at a time.
Give him first place in your life
and live as he wants you to.

TODAY

Ephesians 3:20. Psalm 24:1. Psalm 50:10, 11. Matthew 6:34, 33.

24

Treat others as you want them to treat you.

Practice tenderhearted mercy and kindness to others.

Those you help will be glad not only because of your generous gifts to themselves and to others, but they will praise God for this proof that your deeds are as good as your doctrine.

And they will pray for you with deep fervor and feeling because of the wonderful grace of God shown through you.

TODAY _____

_____

Luke 6:31.   Colossians 3:12.   2 Corinthians 9:13, 14.

DECEMBER

How much God loves us. . . .

God showed how much he loved
us by sending his only Son into
this wicked world to bring to us
eternal life through his death. In
this act we see what real love is.

Long ago, even before he
made the world, God chose us to
be his very own, through what
Christ would do for us; he decided
then to make us holy in his
eyes, without a single fault—we
who stand before him covered
with his love. His unchanging plan
has always been to adopt us into
his own family by sending Jesus
Christ to die for us. And he did
this because he wanted to!

_____ **TODAY**

_____

_____

1 John 4:16. 1 John 4:9, 10. Ephesians 1:4, 5.

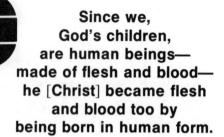

DECEMBER

23

**Since we,
God's children,
are human beings—
made of flesh and blood—
he [Christ] became flesh
and blood too by
being born in human form.**

These are the facts concerning the birth of Jesus Christ: His mother, Mary, was engaged to be married to Joseph. But while she was still a virgin she became pregnant by the Holy Spirit. Then Joseph, her fiancé, being a man of stern principle, decided to break the engagement but to do it quietly, as he didn't want to publicly disgrace her.

As he lay awake considering this, he fell into a dream, and saw an angel standing beside him. "Joseph, son of David," the angel said, "don't hesitate to take Mary as your wife! For the child within her has been conceived by the Holy Spirit. And she will have a Son, and you shall name him Jesus (meaning 'Savior'), for he will save his people from their sins."

TODAY _____

_____

Hebrews 2:14.   Matthew 1:18, 19, 20, 21.

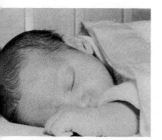

**And she [Mary] gave birth
to her first child, a son.
She wrapped him in a blanket
and laid him in a manger,
because there was no room
for them in the village inn.**

That night some shepherds were
in the fields outside the village,
guarding their flocks of sheep.
Suddenly an angel appeared
among them, and the landscape
shone bright with the glory of
the Lord. They were badly
frightened, but the angel
reassured them.

"Don't be afraid!" he said. "I
bring you the most joyful news
ever announced, and it is for
everyone! The Savior—yes, the
Messiah, the Lord—has been
born tonight in Bethlehem!"

_____ **TODAY**

_____

Luke 2:7. Luke 2:8, 9, 10, 11.

**Thank God
for his Son—
his Gift
too wonderful
for words.**

Shout with joy before the Lord,
O earth! Obey him gladly; come
before him, singing with joy. Go
through his open gates with
great thanksgiving; enter his courts
with praise. Give thanks to him
and bless his name.

For unto us a Child is born;
unto us a Son is given; and the
government shall be upon his
shoulder. These will be his royal
titles: "Wonderful," "Counselor,"
"The Mighty God," "The Everlasting
Father," "The Prince of Peace."

TODAY _____

_____

_____

2 Corinthians 9:15.   Psalm 100:1, 2, 4.   Isaiah 9:6.

DECEMBER

26

You shall name him Jesus (meaning "Savior"), for he will save his people from their sins.

He was wounded and bruised for *our* sins. He was chastised that we might have peace; he was lashed—and we were healed! *We* are the ones who strayed away like sheep! *We,* who left God's paths to follow our own. Yet God laid on *him* the guilt and sins of every one of us! He was oppressed and he was afflicted, yet he never said a word. From prison and trial they led him away to his death.

He came . . . to put away the power of sin forever by dying for us.

In this man Jesus, there is forgiveness for your sins!

TODAY _____

_____

Matthew 1:21.   Isaiah 53:5, 6, 7, 8.   Hebrews 9:26.   Acts 13:38.

God . . .
full of kindness
through Christ.

God declares us "not guilty" of
offending him if we trust in
Jesus Christ, who in his kindness
freely takes away our sins. For
God sent Christ Jesus to take the
punishment for our sins and to
end all God's anger against us. He
used Christ's
blood and our
faith as the means of
saving us from his wrath.
In this way he was being
entirely fair, even though he did
not punish those who sinned in
former times. For he was looking
forward to the time when Christ
would come and take away those sins.

Because of his kindness you have
been saved through trusting
Christ. And even trusting is not of
yourselves; it too is a gift from God.

_____ **TODAY**

_____

_____

1 Peter 5:10. Romans 3:24, 25. Ephesians 2:8.

**Christ became
a human being
and lived here
on earth.**

Your attitude should be the kind
that was shown us by Jesus
Christ, who, though he was God,
did not demand and cling to his
rights as God, but laid aside his
mighty power and glory, taking
the disguise of a slave and
becoming like men. And he
humbled himself even further,
going so far as actually to die a
criminal's death on a cross.

_____ **TODAY**

_____

_____

John 1:14.   Philippians 2:5, 6, 7, 8.

**Christ said . . .
"Here I am.
I have come
to give my life."**

Yet it was because of this that
God raised him up to the heights
of heaven and gave him a name
which is above every other name,
that at the name of Jesus every
knee shall bow in heaven and on
earth and under the earth, and
every tongue shall confess that
Jesus Christ is Lord, to the glory of
God the Father.

TODAY _____

_____

_____

Hebrews 10:8, 9. Philippians 2:9, 10, 11.

Stay always
within the boundaries
where God's love
can reach and bless you.

Let me say this one more thing:
Fix your thoughts on what is
true and good and right. Think
about things that are pure and
lovely, and dwell on the fine, good
things in others. Think about all
you can praise God for and be
glad about.

Keep on believing the things you
have been taught.

The Lord will stay with you as
long as you stay with him!
Whenever you look for him, you
will find him.

TODAY _____

_____

_____

Jude 21. Philippians 4:8. 2 Timothy 3:14. 2 Chronicles 15:2.

DECEMBER 31

**The
Lord
lives on
forever.**

The First and Last, the
    Living One who died,
Who is now alive
    forevermore.
He is robed in majesty and
    strength.
The world is his throne.
His power is incredible.
O Lord, you have reigned
    from prehistoric times, from
    the everlasting past.
Yours is the mighty power
    and glory and victory and
    majesty.

TODAY _____

_____

_____

Psalm 9:7.   Revelation 1:18.   Psalm 93:1, 2.   Nahum 1:3.   Psalm 93:2.
1 Chronicles 29:11

VERSES TO REMEMBER

[Write your own]

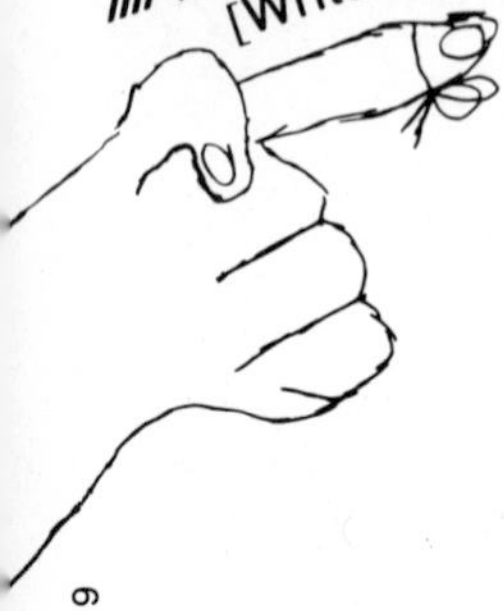

Karen Jongsma, age 9

_____
_____
_____
_____
_____
_____
_____
_____
_____
_____
_____
_____
_____
_____
_____
_____
_____
_____
_____
_____
_____

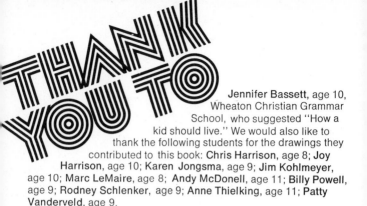

THANK YOU TO

Jennifer Bassett, age 10, Wheaton Christian Grammar School, who suggested "How a kid should live." We would also like to thank the following students for the drawings they contributed to this book: **Chris Harrison**, age 8; **Joy Harrison**, age 10; **Karen Jongsma**, age 9; **Jim Kohlmeyer**, age 10; **Marc LeMaire**, age 8; **Andy McDonell**, age 11; **Billy Powell**, age 9; **Rodney Schlenker**, age 9; **Anne Thielking**, age 11; **Patty Vanderveld**, age 9.

Bruce Anspach from Editorial Photocolor Archives: January 20

Alan (Wim) Auceps: January 21; June 25

Steve Barr: January 24; May 11, 30; June 18; October 6 *(top)*; December 11

Marion Berstein/EPA: February 22; September 22; December 28

Randy Birkey: February 8

Jonathan Blocher: May 31

Tim Botts: February 25; March 27; July 13; December 24

Daniel Brody from EPA: page vi *(top left)*; January 25; May 17; August 11; October 2

Judith C. Bryson: April 17; October 18, 21; December 15

James Carroll from EPA: April 4; June 7; August 17; December 3, 13

John Chao: January 14 *(left)*, 15; April 23; August 12; December 16

Christian Service Brigade: April 28 *(bottom left)*; May 23 *(center)*; November 24; December 4

Bob Combs: page ii *(right)*; page iii *(left)*; July 14, 18; August 28; September 26; October 3 *(left)*, 6 *(bottom)*, 24

Kenneth DeJong: May 13

Editorial Photocolor Archives: October 28

Rohn Engh: back cover *(right)*; page ii *(left)*; January 2, 6, 8, 12, 29, 31; February 2, 10, 14, 20, 26, 27, 28; March 3, 18, 24; April 8, 30; May 24; June 8, 10; July 3 *(top left)*, 4, 7; August 5, 24; September 2, 6, 17; October 4

Ted Feder from EPA: November 2

D. W. Funt/EPA: back cover *(spine)*; January 1

Helen Gorges: December 20

Berne Greene from EPA: February 29; May 28; August 26

HJM Photos: January 22; March 16, 31; April 1; May 5, 20, 22; June 27, 30; August 4, 14 *(left)*; September 13, 28; October 3 *(right)*, 11; November 26; December 8, 26